ALL together NOW

for aGes 4-12

D1591751

13 Sunday school lessons when you have kids of all ages in one room

 **LOIS KEFFER**
Author of **ALL-IN-ONE SUNDAY SCHOOL**

 **Group**
Loveland, Colorado
group.com

Group resources really work!

This Group resource incorporates our R.E.A.L. approach to ministry. It reinforces a growing friendship with Jesus, encourages long-term learning, and results in life transformation, because it's

Relational
Learner-to-learner interaction enhances learning and builds Christian friendships.

Experiential
What learners experience through discussion and action sticks with them up to 9 times longer than what they simply hear or read.

Applicable
The aim of Christian education is to equip learners to be both hearers and doers of God's Word.

Learner-based
Learners understand and retain more when the learning process takes into consideration how they learn best.

All Together Now

Volume 1 — FALL

Visit our website: **group.com**

Unless otherwise indicated, all Scripture quotations are taken from the *Holy Bible*, New Living Translation, copyright © 1996, 2004, 2007. Used by permission of Tyndale House Publishers, Inc., Carol Stream, Illinois 60188. All rights reserved.

Credits
Author: Lois Keffer
Editors: Christine Yount Jones, Jennifer Hooks, and Lee Sparks
Chief Creative Officer: Joani Schultz
Cover Designer: Jeff Spencer
Interior Designer: Jean Bruns
Production Artist: Suzi Jensen
Illustrator: Matt Wood

ISBN: 978-0-7644-7803-1
Printed in the United States of America.
10 9 8 7 6   21 20 19 18 17

Table of Contents

Introduction 5
Active Learning in Combined Classes 7
How to Get Started With *All Together Now* 8
Quick-Grab Activities—Plan in a Can 9

THE LESSONS

1. Princess of Egypt 11

An Egyptian Princess Raises Young Moses—Exodus 1:1–2:15; Mark 5:36
★ *Keep hoping in God, even when times are hard.*

2. The Reluctant Prince 21

Moses Hesitates to Lead the Israelites—Exodus 2:16–4:29; Hebrews 4:16
★ *When God gives us a job, he'll always give us the help we need.*

3. The Duel Begins 32

God Sends Plagues on Egypt—Exodus 7:10–10:20; Ephesians 6:10
★ *God is bigger and morc powerful than anyone.*

4. The God of Light and Life 44

The Passover—Exodus 10:21–12:50; 1 John 1:5, 7
★ *God takes care of us.*

5. Standoff at the Red Sea 53

God Stops the Egyptians at the Red Sea—Exodus 13:17–15:21; Psalm 46:10
★ *God helps us when we're in trouble.*

6. Mumble, Grumble 63

God Provides Water, Manna, and Quail—Exodus 15:22–16:36; John 6:1-35
★ *God wants us to be connected to him and trust him for our daily needs.*

7. Carried on Wings of Love 74

God's Love Story With Israel—Exodus 19; Galatians 3:6-9, 26-29
★ *God has lovingly brought us to him.*

8. The Covenant 82
God Gives the Ten Commandments—Exodus 19:10–20:21; Matthew 22:35-40
★ *God gave us laws to guide and protect us.*

9. The God We Can't See 95
Fearing Moses' Long Absence, the People Worship Idols—Exodus 32; John 4:21-24
★ *God wants us to worship him even though we can't see him.*

10. Enough Already! 107
The People Offer Gifts to Build the Tabernacle—Exodus 25:1-9;
35:20-29; 36:4-6; 2 Corinthians 9:7-8
★ *God wants us to give him our best.*

11. Building God's Holy Tent 119
The People Build the Tabernacle—Exodus 25:8–28:42; 30:1–31:11;
35:25-26; 36:1-2; 37–38; Ephesians 2:10
★ *Every gift God gives is special.*

12. The Tabernacle and Jesus' Sacrifice 128
God's Presence Fills the Tabernacle—Exodus 39:32–40:36; Hebrews 9:1-12
★ *Jesus is the perfect, once-and-for-all sacrifice for our sins.*

13. Exodus Journeys 137
God Saves and Delivers His People—Exodus 3:7-12; Hebrews 9:11-12
★ *God leads us to grow closer to him.*

All Together Now

Introduction

Dear Friend in Children's Ministry,

Welcome to *All Together Now, Volume 1!* Are you ready for a hair-raising journey through Exodus with your 4- to 12-year-olds?

Every pass through Exodus for me is full of goose bumps, holy moments, and silent awe as the King of heaven takes on Pharaoh, the most powerful ruler on earth, and defeats him before the trembling and long-oppressed Hebrews.

Before I open my Bible to this dramatic and formative account of the nation of Israel, I rub my hands together in anticipation and say, "Oh boy—here we go!" For no matter how many times I read these biblical accounts, they still beckon with luminous images of a frowning Pharaoh, standing among trappings of power and luxury, doing his worst to God's sweating, laboring people who keep multiplying no matter how they're oppressed. I see a ragged prince return unflinching for a showdown that might as well be called "High Noon" and the Hebrews tensely following instructions for the late-night Passover meal, carefully painting the blood of a perfect lamb on their door posts as instructed, wondering what'll happen next. The scene crescendos with a midnight escape resulting in nearly 2 million former slaves pinned against an impassable body of water with only Moses and shimmering sand separating them from the flying hooves of the war horses of an enraged Pharaoh...and we're just getting started!

God's stated purpose? "I will claim you as my own people, and I will be your God. Then you will know that I am the Lord your God who has freed you from your oppression in Egypt" (Exodus 6:7). And again, "When I raise my powerful hand and bring out the Israelites, the Egyptians will know that I am the Lord" (Exodus 7:5).

Throughout this amazing journey, kids will see how each of these lessons God taught his people so long ago falls with zip-line accuracy into important truths of the New Testament—and into their daily lives!

Keep the following props on hand to enhance the palace and desert settings of your lessons:

- silky scarves and robes
- artificial palm trees
- shiny blue fabric to represent water
- Loreena McKennitt's album, *An Ancient Muse* (available on iTunes or on CD)

Then gather your kindergarteners through sixth-graders for 13 weeks of life-changing adventure. After experiencing standoffs with mighty kings, rumblings and fireworks at the mountain of God, grumbling in the desert, the building of the Tabernacle, and God's indwelling presence, your kids will never be the same.

Lois Keffer

Active Learning in Combined Classes

Research shows people remember most of what they do but only a small percentage of what they hear—which means kids don't do their best learning sitting around a table talking! They need to be involved in lively activities that help bring home the truth of the lesson. Active learning involves teaching through experiences—experiences that help kids understand important principles, messages, and ideas.

Active learning is a discovery process that helps children internalize the truth as it unfolds. Kids don't sit and listen as a teacher tells them what to think and believe—they find out for themselves. Teachers also learn in the process!

Each active-learning experience in this book is followed by questions that encourage kids to share their feelings about what just happened. Further discussion questions help kids interpret their feelings and decide how this truth affects their lives. The final part of each lesson challenges kids to decide what they'll do with what they've learned—how they'll apply it to their lives during the coming week.

How do kids feel about active learning? They love it! Sunday school becomes exciting, slightly unpredictable, and more relevant and life-changing than ever before. So move the table aside, gather your props, and prepare for some unique and memorable learning experiences!

Active learning works beautifully in combined classes. Whether the group is playing a game or acting out a Bible story, kids of all ages can participate on an equal level. You don't need to worry about reading levels and writing skills. Everyone gets a chance to make important contributions to class activities and discussions.

These simple classroom tips will help you get your combined class off to a smooth start:

☐ When kids form groups, aim for an equal balance of older and younger kids in each group. Encourage the older kids to act as coaches to help younger ones get in the swing of each activity.

☐ In "pair-share," everyone works with a partner. When it's time to report to the whole group, each person tells his or her partner's response. This simple technique teaches kids to listen and to cooperate with each other.

☐ If an activity calls for reading or writing, pair young nonreaders with older kids who can lend their skills. Older kids enjoy the esteem-boost that comes with acting as a mentor, and younger kids appreciate getting special attention and broadening their skills.

☐ Don't worry too much about discussion going over the heads of younger children. They'll be stimulated by what they hear the older kids saying. You may be surprised to find some of the most insightful discussion literally coming "out of the mouths of babes."

☐ Make it a point to give everyone—not just those who are academically or athletically gifted—a chance to shine. Affirm kids for their cooperative attitudes when you see them working well together and encouraging each other.

☐ Keep in mind kids may give unexpected answers. That's okay. When kids give "wrong" answers, don't correct them. Say something like: "That's interesting. Let's look at it from another viewpoint." Then ask for ideas from other kids. If you correct their answers, most kids will soon stop offering them.

How to Get Started With All Together Now

TEACHING STAFF

When you combine Sunday school classes, teachers get a break! Teachers who would normally be teaching in your 4- to 12-year-old age groups may want to take turns. Or ask teachers to sign up for the Sundays they'll be available to teach.

LESSONS

The lessons in the *All Together Now* series are grouped by quarter—fall, winter, spring, and summer—but each lesson can also stand on its own.

PREPARATION

Each week you'll need to gather the easy-to-find props in the You'll Need section and photocopy the reproducible handouts. Add to that a careful read of the lesson and Scripture passages, and you're ready to go!

Quick-Grab Activities—Plan in a Can

By Cynthia Crane and Sharon Stratmoen
Reprinted by permission of Children's Ministry Magazine. © Group Publishing, Inc. All rights reserved.

It's Sunday morning and you've just finished your entire lesson. You check the clock, and although the service should be ending, you hear no music, see no parents coming down the hall. What you do hear is your senior pastor, still excited about the message. And then you quickly begin trying to figure out what you're going to do with a room full of kids and no lesson left.

You need a survival kit. A bucket of backup, a plan in a can. So we've created two kits you can build on your own and store in your room. When you have extra time with kids, don't sweat it—just pull out your plan in a can and get busy!

In case you're wondering, Why call it a can? Why not a box or a bin or a bucket? For those times when you're worrying whether you'll be able to keep kids' attention and bust their boredom, the name is a sweet reminder that yes, you can!

PLAN IN A CAN: Games Galore!

. . . .

THE INGREDIENTS

☐ Faithful Faces cards (printed photos, poster board, adhesive, and a laminator or clear adhesive vinyl) held together with a rubber band

☐ sidewalk chalk

☐ Christian music CDs for kids

☐ black-light lamp

☐ 2 large happy-face images

☐ 2 colors of plastic clothespins (enough for 3 per child; available at dollar stores)

FAITHFUL FACES ▸▸ Kids love the Memory Game, where shuffled cards are laid out facedown in a grid and kids try to find matching cards by turning over two at a time. (If they don't get a match, they turn the cards back facedown and the next person goes. If they do get a match, they get another turn.) So why not capitalize on this fun game to model and reinforce the important faithful faces in kids' lives? Just take pictures of the kids in your class, missionaries in your church, Bible friends you've been learning about, families you're praying for, and people in your congregation. Then whip up your own version of the game.

Use photo paper or regular printer paper to print out two of each photo, and mount them on poster board. Run the poster board through a laminator or apply clear adhesive vinyl, and you've got a game worth talking about. Kids will love finding their friends. And when they get a match, throw in a little challenge by giving them an extra point if they can remember names and other details about the person on the card.

SIDEWALK CHALK OF TODAY'S TALK ▸▸ Form groups of two to six, and hand out sidewalk chalk. You can have as many or as few groups as you have sidewalks for. Have groups work together to draw one picture on concrete that says something about the day's Bible story. When parents pick up their kids, you get a huge blessing: The kids tell their parents what they learned without being prompted. As a bonus, take photos of kids and their drawings for a quick recap to start off the following week's lesson. You can even make a month-in-review bulletin board starring your kids as the teachers.

MUSIC FREEZE ▸▸ If you think an hour is a long time for you, it's like dog years to kids. They have wiggles they've got to get out. So when you have extra time, turn up the music and let kids be as goofy as they want—until the music stops. Then they have to freeze in place. Give this a twist by adding a black light. Changing your environment is a great break from the everyday, and it lets kids know that you always have a few surprises in store.

CLOTHESPIN TAG ▸▸ You can use this game to remind kids that no thief can steal our joy when we go to the Joy Source: God. Place the happy-face images on the floor at opposite ends of a play area. Form two teams, and have each team go to one happy face. Assign each team a color of clothespin. Pin three clothespins to the back of each child's clothing above the waist. The goal of the game is for each team to try to steal the other team's clothespins and drop them on their own team's happy face. Play music to signal "go." Let kids play for one minute or so, and then turn off the music to signal "stop." After a few starts and stops, end the game, declare the team with the most clothespins as the winner, and then let kids get more "joy" on their backs and play again. When you're done, remind kids that they can always find new joy with God.

PLAN IN A CAN: Craft Creations

THE INGREDIENTS

- ☐ Legos in a resealable bag
- ☐ Moon Sand sculpting sand
- ☐ PlayFoam sculpting material
- ☐ window crayons
- ☐ Window Writers
- ☐ whiteboard markers
- ☐ Magic Nuudles cornstarch building blocks
- ☐ giant chenille pipe cleaners

- ☐ Bendaroos sculpting sticks
- ☐ one-subject notebook
- ☐ colored pencils
- ☐ Glitter Putty
- ☐ construction paper
- ☐ washable markers
- ☐ SuperBalls
- ☐ Christian music CDs for kids

CREATE ▸▸ If you have time to burn as kids are arriving, try this activity. Have kids use Legos building blocks, Moon Sand sculpting sand, PlayFoam sculpting material, Window Writers, or whiteboard markers to create a symbol of something that happened during the week. Then have kids show their creations as they say: "Hi, my name is _____, and I created this _____, because last week _____."

RESPOND ▸▸ Let kids use any craft supplies from the can to create a symbol of what the day's lesson meant to them. For instance, kids can draw a picture or write how they'll apply the point to life, using the windows, a whiteboard, or paper. Or they might choose to create a symbol that reminds them of what they learned, using giant chenille pipe cleaners or Bendaroos sculpting sticks. Invite kids to share what their creations represent.

PRAY ▸▸ Create a class prayer journal with a notebook for kids to write prayer notes in. Have kids all write their names on the cover because the journal belongs to all of them. Take out the journal throughout the year. Encourage kids to take turns writing their prayers or notes using colored pencils. If kids are stumped, give them prayer prompts such as "I thank God for..." "I need help with..." and "I pray for..." Close your time with prayer, and include requests from the prayer journal.

CHILL ▸▸ Give kids Glitter Putty, SuperBalls, or simply space. Play Christian music and let kids just "chill" as they quietly listen. Use the following tactile treats to help them focus on the music. As they listen, let them squish Glitter Putty between their fingers, play with SuperBalls, or simply relax on the floor at least 5 feet away from anyone else and close their eyes.

All Together Now

Princess of Egypt

LESSON AIM

To encourage kids to ★ *keep hoping in God, even when times are hard.*

OBJECTIVES

Kids will

✓ perform a discouraging task, like the Hebrew slaves did in Egypt,

✓ hear the princess of Egypt tell about her son, Moses,

✓ create a model of an Egyptian palace,

✓ form a "mud brick" from cream cheese spread and chow mein noodles, and

✓ pray about discouraging things in their lives.

BIBLE BASIS

 Exodus 1:1—2:15

"Mo-ses, Mo-ses." Can you just hear the drawl of the glamorous actress appealing to Charlton Heston in the old movie *The Ten Commandments*? I always have to laugh at that and then set it aside in my mind before I can begin serious study of this dramatic and formative story of the nation of Israel.

For this lesson we'll hear from the Egyptian princess who adopted Moses. The book of Exodus doesn't give us quite enough historical detail to place these events exactly within

You'll need...

☐ masking tape

☐ package of tissue paper

☐ 2 brooms

☐ 2 buckets

☐ 2 dustpans

☐ volunteer to play the princess of Egypt *(optional)*

☐ photocopy of the "Princess Script" (pp. 15-16)

☐ costume for the princess of Egypt: silky scarves and robe, jewelry, crown, jeweled sandals

☐ fancy cushions for the princess of Egypt to sit on

☐ "Incantation" from Loreena McKennitt's album *An Ancient Muse* and CD player *(optional)*

☐ photocopies of "Pharaoh's Palace" handout (p. 18)

☐ scissors

☐ glue sticks

☐ cream cheese spread*

☐ chow mein noodles*

☐ plastic knives

☐ small plates

* Always check for allergies before serving snacks.

the reign of a certain Pharaoh. We do know that the Hebrews had multiplied to such a degree that the Pharaoh considered them a threat, so much so that he subjugated them to slavery and ordered their midwives to kill all the baby boys.

Can you imagine, in this setting, a princess coming home and saying, "Hey, Dad, you'll never guess what I did today! I adopted a baby Hebrew boy...you know, one of those babies you ordered to be killed!" We hear nothing more about this princess after the well-known biblical account of her compassion for the Hebrew infant: how she hired his own mother to raise him until he was weaned and then took him into the palace as her own son. Had she only known she was drawing from the water the very individual who would, as a man, overthrow another Pharaoh and lead all the Hebrew slaves to freedom!

During the years of the Hebrews' desperate suffering under Pharaoh, God already had a solution in the works. There was a little boy with his mom, a young man in the palace, and then a fugitive in faraway Midian whom God was grooming for the task of liberator. The groaning Israelites could see no evidence of God's work on their behalf, but he was working nevertheless.

📖 **Mark 5:36**

"Don't be afraid; just have faith." Jesus made this statement to a man whose situation was even more desperate than that of the Israelites: He'd just been informed that his daughter was dead. But the man kept believing, and he led Jesus to his home where wailing mourners greeted them. There Jesus lovingly called the child back to life. In the most desperate of circumstances, those who put their faith in Jesus always have hope.

UNDERSTANDING YOUR KIDS

Kids live very much in the moment. A treat or privilege denied now seems like the disaster of a lifetime. It's important for them to see that even when they're not looking, God is at work in their lives and that today's tragedy may well turn into next month's golden moment, because God always has our best in mind. Use this lesson to encourage kids to ★ *keep hoping in God, even when times are hard.*

All Together Now

ATTENTION GRABBER

A Mean Master

Ask:

• **What's fun about making a big mess?**

• **What's fun—or not so fun—about cleaning up a big mess?**

Say: **Well, today you're going to get a chance to do both, because you're going to be like God's slaves in Egypt.**

First, I need you to form two groups.

Run a masking tape line down the middle of the room between the two groups.

Give each group half a package of tissue paper and a bucket.

Say: **Here's the fun part. You get to tear the tissue paper into as many tiny pieces as you can and throw the pieces in the air for two minutes. Make as big a mess as you can.** Allow time. Then give each group a broom and dustpan.

Say: **Unfortunately, the time has come to clean up your mess. Work together to get every tiny piece of tissue paper back in your bucket. Let's see which group finishes first. Don't be lazy slaves. Go! Go! Go!**

When kids have finished, say: **I am the all-powerful Pharaoh, king of Egypt, the most powerful ruler in the world. Here's the bad news: I'm just plain mean to my slaves.**

Cross your arms and give the kids a terrible royal glare.

Say: **I've seen the way you lazy slaves stand around all day. I'm going to double your workload and take away your tools.**

Throw the tissue paper bits out from each bucket and then instruct the kids to pick them up, but take the brooms and dustpans away. As kids work, walk around the room saying, "Work harder! Go faster! Work harder! Go faster!"

Finally, when kids have collected all the paper bits in their buckets, gather everyone in a circle on the floor.

Ask:

• **What did you think of me as a master?**

• **How would it feel to have to work for me all week without getting paid anything?**

• **How would your life be different if everyone in your family had to be my slaves for the rest of your lives?**

Say: **This is what life was like for God's people in our Bible story. Today's the first step of our journey through the Old**

Teacher Tip

If possible, ensure there is an equal number of older and younger children in each group.

Testament book of Exodus. In this lesson we'll see that even when things were at their worst for God's people, God was already at work on their behalf.

BIBLE EXPLORATION

Princess of Egypt (Exodus 1:1–2:15)

Before class, arrange for a volunteer to play the princess of Egypt. Since Moses was 40 when he left Egypt, she'd be an older woman at this point, but for purposes of our story an actress of any age will do. If possible, have her waiting in a different room from the one where you meet. Make the setup as simple or elaborate as you like. Dress the princess in colorful silky fabrics with elaborate jewelry and sandals. If you wish, add heavy triangular eyeliner, typical of Egyptian paintings. Artificial palms and the track "Incantation" from Loreena McKennitt's *An Ancient Muse* album can further add to the scene. Have the princess seated on pillows on the floor.

Or, if you prefer, slip on costume pieces and play the role of the princess yourself. Practice reading or telling the story from the "Princess Script" on pages 15-16.

Gather kids in a circle and say: **I have such a surprise for our Bible story that I'm not sure you're ready for it. I mean, this is a *really* big surprise.**

Today we're going to meet the princess of Egypt. In fact, she's invited us to sneak into Pharaoh's palace to hear what she has to say. I hardly have to tell you what a dangerous mission this is. But the last person we want to see is Pharaoh himself—he's exceptionally mean. So if you run into this really royal-looking guy with a crown, duck and run for your life! We have to make it to the princess' chambers without being seen. Think we can do that?

Lead the kids through the hall as if you're heading for a secret destination. Dodge from corner to corner, encouraging everyone to be whisper-quiet. Make your final destination the place where the princess is waiting, or your own room if you're playing the part of the princess.

All Together Now

Princess Script

Quickly! Come join me! Did anyone see you in the palace hallways on the way to my chambers? No? Good! You see, what I'm about to tell you is a big problem between me and my father, Pharaoh. It's been a problem for many, many years. Ever since I found that little basket floating in the river.

(Move to a different location.)

It was so long ago. I took several servants and went down to the river to take a bath. Just as I was getting into the water, I noticed a strange thing—a covered basket floating in the tall reeds by the river's edge. I sent one of my servant girls to get it. Inside was a baby boy—a perfect little baby boy, and he was crying.

(Imitate receiving a baby, rocking him, and giving soothing words to calm his crying.)

I knew right away this must have been one of the little Hebrew babies. The Hebrews—the Israelites—are foreigners who've lived among us for hundreds of years. My father hates them. He's made them slaves and makes them work harder than you can imagine. If there's a war, my father thinks they might turn against us.

I feel differently about the Hebrews. Some of my dearest servants are Hebrew, and I love them. They're like family to me. I'd never do anything to hurt them.

(Change location and then continue.)

Finally my father, the great Pharaoh of Egypt, gave a terrible order. He commanded that all Hebrew baby boys be killed. The girls could live, but the baby boys must be killed.

(Pause to reflect on the enormous evil of Pharaoh's order.)

Isn't that awful? If the families didn't kill their own baby boys, our soldiers would go through their towns and kill them. I was sure that this beautiful little boy I'd found in the river was Hebrew. His mother must have set him afloat hoping that an Egyptian would find him and keep him alive. And that's exactly what I decided to do.

Published in *All Together Now, Volume 1* by Group Publishing, Inc., 1515 Cascade Ave., Loveland, CO 80538.

15

No sooner had I pulled the crying baby from the river than an older Hebrew girl came running up and asked if I'd like her to find someone to nurse him. Of course I accepted her offer. I named the little boy Moses and sent him off to be raised in a Hebrew home until he was about 3 years old.

(Imitate giving a child to another home and then excitement at his return.)

Oh, I was so delighted the day Moses came back to me at the palace! He was so strong. He was raised with all the other princes in the palace and he made me so proud.

(Pause and reflect.)

I decided to tell Moses when he was still young that he was different from the other princes. He wasn't Egyptian, but Hebrew. Now I don't know if that was such a good idea. If I'd just kept his secret, we might not have the trouble we do now.

(Change locations and continue.)

Moses was always curious about his own people. When he was old enough, he'd wander away from the palace to see the Hebrew people working. He saw cruel masters beating them if they didn't get enough done. He saw how different his life in the palace was from theirs.

One day when Moses saw a taskmaster being cruel to a Hebrew slave, he just couldn't take it any more. He got so angry that he killed the cruel taskmaster. Then he had to run away before Pharaoh had him killed.

That was a week ago. I don't know where Moses went or when he'll be back. I may have lost my beautiful Hebrew son forever.

Now you'd better sneak out of the palace before anyone finds you here. If you run into any guards on the way, don't say anything about Moses! Just explain that you had a special meeting with the princess.

Now hurry! My father sometimes comes to this part of the palace to see whether I have any information about Moses. Hurry—and be safe!

After the Bible story with the princess of Egypt, sneak with kids back to your room. Say: **Pharaoh was the most powerful ruler on earth at the time, but privately he was scared of the growing number of Hebrews.**

Ask:

• **What made Moses different from the other princes at the palace?**

• **Suppose you lived in a rich palace with every luxury, but your family back home was very poor. What would you do?**

• **What do you think of Moses killing the taskmaster who was beating a Hebrew slave?**

LIFE APPLICATION
. . . .
Help Is on the Way

Say: **Because Moses was adopted by an Egyptian princess, he grew up in a luxurious palace. Let's make a model of what that palace might have looked like.**

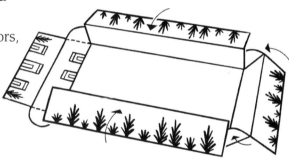

Distribute copies of the "Pharaoh's Palace" handout, scissors, and glue sticks. Show kids how to cut and fold their palace models so the outside walls stand up. Have them glue the tabs on the end pieces between the layers of the outer walls to give the walls stability.

Ask:

• **What details do you notice about the palace?**

• **What kinds of things would be inside a Pharaoh's palace?**

Say: **Moses knew he wasn't an Egyptian—he was Hebrew. Every now and then he wandered out to where his people were working. They had to make bricks from straw and mud and then build huge storage cities out of those bricks.**

Ask:

• **Suppose you'd been in Moses' shoes—you lived in luxury, but you went out and saw your countrymen, members of your own family, treated cruelly. How would you handle that situation?**

The Hebrews had been treated badly for many years, but God didn't want them to give up! God wants us to ★ *keep hoping in him, even when times are hard.* **Even if we can't see it, God already has a solution in mind, and he's working on it!**

Pharaoh's Palace

Make your own model of an Egyptian palace like the one where Moses might have grown up.

1. Cut out the outline of the palace.
2. Fold up the walls to make them stand up.
3. Glue the tabs on the end pieces between the layers of the outer walls.

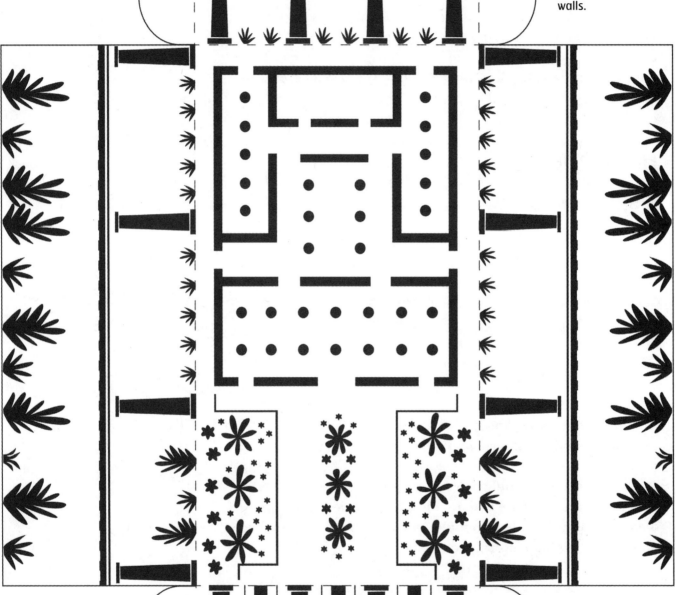

Unfortunately, Moses tried to take things into his own hands. He killed a cruel slave master, and then Pharaoh wanted to kill him. Once he was gone from Egypt, Moses could do nothing to help his people...or so he thought. This was a great turning point in Moses' life so God could prepare him for the job ahead.

COMMITMENT

Brick by Brick

Ask:

• **Tell about a time you felt you were in an impossible situation.**

• **Tell about a time, if ever, you felt like things were so bad you should just give up.**

Share an experience of your own when you waited in difficult circumstances for a long time before God answered your prayers.

Say: **Sometimes people make the mistake of thinking that God doesn't hear their prayers or doesn't care. That's not how it is at all! God gives us these stories in his Word so we'll understand that God wants us to ★ *keep hoping in him, even when times are hard*. We can't always see what God is doing, but we can trust him to be working on an answer to our prayers. He loved his people, the Hebrews, very much and he heard their cries for help. He was already at work on an amazing plan to set them free from slavery. For the time being, their job was to keep hoping in him.**

Set out small plates, cartons of cream cheese spread, and chow mein noodles. Give each child a plastic knife.

Say: **Work together in groups of three to build bricks. Each of you will build one brick on your plate. In our Bible passage today, the Hebrew slaves used straw and mud. The cream cheese spread will be the mud, and the chow mein noodles will be the straw. First put a little pile of chow mein noodles on your plate. Break them into smaller pieces to make straw. As your break them, take turns telling your group of three about a hard situation you've been praying about for a long time.**

When kids have made their straw, say: **Now add cream cheese mud to your plate and form your pile of mud and straw into a nice, solid brick.**

. . . .

Brick Prayers

When kids have their bricks formed, have kids take turns sharing a concern and praying for one another in their groups before they enjoy their brick treats. After a few minutes, say: **Thanks for your participation today! The Hebrew people suffered a lot under Pharaoh. We also have problems that feel overwhelming at times. That's why we** ★ *keep hoping in God, even when times are hard.*

The Reluctant Prince

LESSON AIM

To help kids believe that ★ *when God gives us a job, he'll always give us the help we need.*

OBJECTIVES

Kids will

✓ accomplish tasks that are impossible without help,

✓ take part in an interactive story about Moses' job assignment in Egypt,

✓ make treasure bag reminders about God giving us the help we need, and

✓ commit to courageously accepting the jobs God has for them and looking for his help.

BIBLE BASIS

 Exodus 2:16—4:29

When it comes to face-to-face conversations with God, it's interesting to compare the styles of two Old Testament heroes: Abraham and Moses. Abraham, when called to leave civilization as he knew it and travel to no man's land, bowed low before God, got a caravan together, and took off. Through his long years of waiting for a child, Abraham "believed the Lord, and the Lord counted him as righteousness" (Genesis 15:6).

In contrast to Abraham, when God told Moses to go back into Egypt to bring the suffering Hebrews out, Moses had an

You'll need...

☐ Bibles

☐ balloons*

☐ masking tape

☐ large garbage bag

☐ Bible-times costume, such as a robe and sandals

☐ squirt bottle of water

☐ photocopies of the "Grace and Mercy Bags" handout (p. 29) on heavy paper

☐ scissors

☐ markers

☐ glue sticks

☐ paper punch

☐ lightweight string or raffia

☐ M&Ms candies**

* Warning! Choking hazard— Children under 8 yrs. can choke or suffocate on uninflated or broken balloons. Adult supervision required. Keep uninflated balloons from children. Discard broken balloons at once. Balloons may contain latex.

** Always check for allergies before serving snacks.

excuse for not following every command, a "but-what-if" for every promise. In fact, Moses' back talk ignited God's anger to "burn against him" (Exodus 4:14, NIV). I hope he wasn't standing too near that bush! God gave Moses detailed plans, leading him by the hand in this mission as if he were a little child. But Moses, without even thinking about it, was sure that God's idea was all wrong.

Perhaps it was because Moses had lived in Pharaoh's palace and knew the absolute power that Pharaoh and his minions used to rule their empire. Perhaps it was because long ago he had resigned himself to the hopelessness of the situation. Who can say what caused Moses to so boldly doubt God during their personal encounter?

It's possible that Moses was just beginning to get an idea of how big God is. He knew firsthand about Pharaoh's might. But perhaps this was his first encounter with the true and living God, the one God of Israel whose name was so holy it couldn't be spoken. This encounter on Mount Horeb was God's get-to-know-you meeting with Moses, who was so overwhelmed by the challenges of the situation that he couldn't begin to grasp who was calling him.

However, the truth is that we tend to act the same as Moses at times. "But my job is going away." "But I just heard the 'C' word from my doctor." "But my kids are always fighting." "But suddenly I have to move across the country." The distractions in life, both big and small, can prevent us from seeing that the one doing the calling is *the God of the universe!* This is the same God who made us and calls us beloved. This is the same God who promises to supply all our needs according to his riches in glory. (This message rubs closely to the fabric of my everyday life. I write now in the aftermath of a brain injury. Words don't come like they used to.)

It's no small thing to receive a call from God. When it's a *true call,* God will always give us the help we need.

📖 Hebrews 4:16

Jesus himself received a difficult call—one to the cross. He understands our misgivings and our cries for help in the midst of what seem to be overwhelming situations. Jesus, through his death and resurrection, has become our great high priest. He acts on our behalf like an usher, taking us right to the very throne of God where all our needs will be met.

All Together Now

UNDERSTANDING YOUR KIDS

Kids have always faced troubles and problems. As adults, "revisionism" can cloud memories of our own childhood challenges. Keep in mind that kids face obstacles and problems that are very real and deep for them. School pressures, troubles at home, bullying, taunts in the hallways, and neighborhood threats can each add up to as big an obstacle to children as Pharaoh was to Moses.

During these formative years in the early grades, kids need to understand beyond a shadow of a doubt that their God who is unseen is a far greater power than the forces in their lives that are seen. Face it—this is a tough truth even for the most faithful adults to hold in mind. Use this lesson to teach your kids that ★ *when God gives us a job, he'll always give us the help we need* to accomplish it.

THE LESSON »

ATTENTION GRABBER

You've Got a Friend

Before class, inflate several balloons. You'll need approximately half as many balloons as there are kids in your class, plus a few extra. Place masking tape lines on the floor of your room as far apart as space allows.

Say: **I hope you're up for a challenge, because I've got a good one! Who wants to go first?**

Choose a willing child. Hand him or her a balloon and say: **Your challenge is to start at this line, walk all the way to the other line and back to this line balancing the balloon on your head. Oh, by the way, you may not use your hands at all. Once I place it on your head, you need to balance it. Does that make sense?**

Have the child repeat the instructions back to you.

After the first child fails, allow several other children to try. You may want to let all the kids try and fail.

Say: **Hmm. We seem to have a problem here.**

Ask:

• **Why could no one complete the challenge?**

Appear to look puzzled for a while. Then brighten up and say: **I have an idea. What if each of you had a partner? Let's see. Pair up with someone close to your own height.**

Now the challenge is still the same. But this time, your partner may touch the balloon with one finger. Only one finger! Which pair wants to try the challenge first?

Pairs will soon discover that if one partner pushes down on the balloon, it'll help keep it on the other partner's head. It's still a tricky challenge, but doable! Give plenty of time for both people in each pair to succeed at the challenge. Then have kids toss their balloons into the garbage bag and sit in a circle for discussion.

Ask:

• **What was different about the first and second time we tried this?**

• **How much did it help to have a partner?**

Say: **I'm going to name some things that might be easy for you or they might be real challenges. If what I mention would be easy, sit still. If what I mention would be a challenge, wave a hand in the air. Here we go.**

All Together Now

✓ taking part in a spelling bee

✓ introducing yourself to someone new in the neighborhood and making him or her feel welcome

✓ drawing a picture of yourself

✓ singing a solo

✓ doing a timed math test

✓ catching a fly ball in a softball game

✓ having a speaking part in a play

✓ standing on your head

✓ writing a story

✓ training a dog

✓ winning a video game

✓ drawing plans for a tree house

Ask:

• **What did you notice about the way everyone answered?**

• **Why were our answers different?**

• **What would you do if God gave you a job that was really, really hard for you?**

Say: **In today's Bible passage, that's exactly what happens to our hero, Moses. Only I'm afraid he doesn't act like much of a hero today. He's absolutely sure he can't handle the challenge God puts before him. So sure, in fact, he actually *talks back to God*. Whoa! But before the end, Moses learns that ★ *when God gives us a job, he'll always give us the help we need* to accomplish it. Let's find out what happens!**

BIBLE EXPLORATION
. . . .

The Reluctant Prince (Exodus 2:16–4:29)

Say: **Pharaoh's daughter had adopted Moses when he was a baby. But the Bible says nothing else about Moses' childhood. When he was a man, Moses got into trouble and ran away—all the way to the land of Midian. There he sat down by a well and...wait. This Bible story will be a lot better if you help me tell it. Please form two groups—boys and girls. I'll read part of the story from the Bible. Then if I point to your group, you act it out. Before we get started, I need someone to be Moses.**

Choose a willing child who'll be expressive at miming Moses' actions in the Bible story. Have the child quickly put on a Bible-times costume and then stand near you.

Here we go.

When Moses arrived in Midian, he sat down beside a well. Now the priest of Midian had seven daughters who came to draw water and fill the water troughs for their father's flocks.

(Have girls pretend to draw water and fill troughs.)

But some other shepherds came and chased them away.

(Have boys chase girls away from troughs.)

So Moses jumped up and rescued the girls from the shepherds.

(Have Moses gather girls and stand as a hero between the girls and the boys.)

Boys, now you're the flocks. Get down on your knees and baa like sheep.

(Let the boys baa for a few moments.)

Then Moses watered their flocks.

(Hand Moses a squirt bottle of water, and have Moses squirt the "flocks" with water.)

Hearing of Moses' kindness, the girls' father, Jethro, invited Moses to dinner.

(Have girls make a circle around Moses.)

The oldest daughter, Zipporah, became Moses' wife.

(Have kids return to their seats.)

Years passed. The Israelite slaves continued to cry out to God for help, and God heard them.

(Have all kids groan.)

Moses worked for his father-in-law tending sheep. Moses took the sheep far into the wilderness to Sinai, the mountain of God.

(Have everyone pile something together to create a mountain. Be safe!)

There the angel of the Lord appeared to him in a blazing fire from the middle of a bush. Moses stared in amazement. It didn't burn up. "This is amazing," Moses said to himself. "Why isn't that bush burning up? I must go see it."

(Have boys link legs and arms together to represent the branches of a large bush. Have girls move around the bush and wave their arms around the bush like flames. Then have girls stop the actions and spread out into a large circle. Moses stays outside the circle. Step into the middle of the circle and continue telling the story.)

When the Lord saw Moses coming to take a closer look, God called to him from the middle of the bush, "Moses! Moses!"

(Tell Moses to say, "Here I am!")

"Do not come any closer," the Lord warned. "Take off your sandals, for you are standing on holy ground. I am the God of your father— the God of Abraham, the God of Isaac, and the God of Jacob." When Moses heard this, he covered his face because he was afraid to look at God.

(Have Moses cover his face.)

Then the Lord told Moses, "I have certainly seen the oppression of my people in Egypt. Yes, I am aware of their suffering. So I have come down to rescue them from the power of the Egyptians. Now go, for I am sending you to Pharaoh. You must lead my people Israel out of Egypt." When God was finished speaking, Moses responded with protests and pleas; he did not want to do as God asked.

(Have Moses repeat these one at time: "Who am I to go back to Pharaoh?" "What if Pharaoh won't listen to me?" "Please send someone else.")

Then the Lord asked Moses, "Who makes a person's mouth? Who decides whether people speak or do not speak, hear or do not hear, see or do not see? Is it not I, the Lord? Now go! I will be with you as you speak, and I will instruct you in what to say." But Moses again pleaded, "Lord, please! Send anyone else." Then the Lord became angry with Moses. "All right," he said. "What about your brother, Aaron the Levite? I know he speaks well. And look! He is on his way to meet you now. He will be delighted to see you. Talk to him, and put the words in his mouth. I will be with both of you as you speak, and I will instruct you both in what to do."

(Have someone be Aaron and go to Moses. Have them give each other high fives. Then have them walk away together.)

Say: **Thank you for your wonderful performances.**

Ask:

• If you could've given Moses advice in the middle of his conversation with God, what would you say to him?

• Why would you have given advice like that?

Say: **Moses really had his doubts. He had decided right from the start that this challenge was too much for him, like the challenge we did with balloons in our opening game. The first time it was just too hard. Then I gave you a friend to help and that made all the difference. Seeing how scared Moses was, God gave him a friend to help. A brother, actually. Because ★ when God gives us a job, he'll always give us the help we need.**

Let's find out how Moses responded to God's last offer of help.

Say: **Moses and Aaron returned to Egypt and called all of the Israelite leaders together. The leaders believed what Moses and Aaron told them and showed them. The leaders knew that God had heard their cries for help.**

Ask:

• Why do you think none of Moses' fears came true?

• How did God's partner system work out?

Say: **★ When God gives us a job, he'll always give us the help we need! That was true for Moses, and it's true for us today. You can count on it!**

LIFE APPLICATION

Grace and Mercy Bags

Say: **God may not talk to us in the desert the way he did to Moses. But God does encourage us to step right into his throne room where the Bible says we will find grace to help us when we need it most.**

Ask:

• Tell about a time you needed God's help.

Say: **Let's make reminders that ★ when God gives us a job, he'll always give us the help we need.**

Distribute copies of the "Grace and Mercy Bags" handout. For extra durability, make copies on heavy paper. Set out scissors, markers, glue sticks, a paper punch, and lengths of lightweight string or raffia.

Demonstrate how to cut out the bag on the solid lines.

Grace and Mercy Bags

This Bible verse reminds us to go to the very throne of God for help when we need it! Now that's something to remember!

1. Cut out the bag on the solid lines.
2. Write your name or draw your portrait on the back inside the frame. Be sure to turn the bag in the right direction!
3. Fold in the tabs on the dotted lines. Run a glue stick over the tabs and press the bag together.
4. Hole punch the circles.

See what your teacher has to put in the bags!

Fold in and glue.

Fold in and glue.

So let us come boldly to the throne of our gracious God. There we will receive his mercy, and we will find grace to help us when we need it most.

Hebrews 4:16

Published in *All Together Now, Volume 1* by Group Publishing, Inc., 1515 Cascade Ave., Loveland, CO 80538.

When kids have their bags cut out, invite a child to read aloud Hebrews 4:16.

Ask:

- **What do you think this verse means?**
- **When and where can you ask God for help?**
- **Why do you think that the great big God who made our gigantic universe is willing to listen to little, tiny people like us anytime, anywhere, about any challenge we're facing?**

Say: **Even though it might sound too good to be true, it's not. Just as God cared about all the people suffering in Israel, God cares about us. Just as God gave Moses everything he needed to be ready for his big job, he'll make sure we have everything we need for the jobs he gives us. Let's do a wave cheer for God!**

Have kids do the wave as they shout, "Y-a-y, God!" Finish with jumping and shouting. Then lead kids back to the craft.

★ *When God gives us a job, he'll always give us the help we need.* **Let's make this treasure bag as a reminder of our open invitation to come to God with our needs. Fold your bag on the dotted lines.**

COMMITMENT

Treasure in the Bag

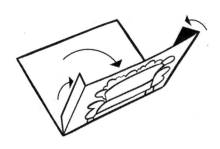

Say: **Before we put the finishing touches on our bags, write your name or draw a picture of yourself on the blank side. That way you'll remember that this verse from the Bible is all about what God wants *you* to do.**

When they have finished drawing, have kids fold in the flaps, carefully rub them with glue, and then fold up the bottom of the bag and seal it. Encourage kids to rub over the seal several times so it remains nice and firm. Have older kids hole-punch the bags through the circles.

Hold a bag of M&Ms candies behind your back, smile conspiratorially, and say: **I just might have a little treasure to go in those bags of yours. Who would like some?**

Pour a few chocolate candies into each bag, and into kids' hands as well.

Say: **Save the treasure in your bags for later—for a time you really need it!**

All Together Now

Give each child a length of string or raffia to loop through the holes in the top of their bags and tie them shut.

Say: **I gave you some sweet treasures for your bag.**

Ask:

- **What does God give you when you go to him for help?**
- **Tell about a time you prayed to God and he helped you.**

Say: **God doesn't always give us easy jobs. Sometimes he asks us to get along with a brother or sister. Or obey our parents without whining or talking back. Sometimes God asks us to tell others about him.**

Ask:

- **Tell about hard jobs God gives you.**
- **How can God help you with those hard jobs?**

Say: **I have a challenge for you. When you go home, show your family the treasure bag you made and tell them what it means. Raise your hand if you accept the challenge.**

I'm sure your family would love to hear about Moses' experiences with God in today's Bible story. Raise your hand if you're willing to accept the challenge of being a Bible storyteller. Now you've got two challenges. And I know God will give you everything you need to do your jobs.

CLOSING

Affirmation Toss

Form two lines so half of the children are facing the other half. Give the kids in one line balloons.

Say: **Sometimes when we're in the middle of a tough challenge, we kind of forget that we can ask God to help. So we're going to do a little balloon toss to help us remember. The person facing you is your partner. People holding the balloons, shout:** ★ *When God gives us a job,* **and then bat the balloon to your partner. People catching the balloons, shout:** *He'll always give us the help we need.* **Let's try that!**

Excellent job. Let's do it a few more times, getting faster and faster!

After a few tosses, have the partners switch roles, with the other partner initiating today's point. Then gather the balloons in the garbage bag. Have the kids gather in a tight circle, make a pile of fists, and break on, "Yay, God!"

Teacher Tip

Show kids how to bat the balloon like a volleyball to make it travel the distance between the two lines. Let younger kids practice a bit.

Teacher Tip

The second phrase may be a little long for some of your younger kids, so remind them if they need it.

The Duel Begins

You'll need...

- ☐ 7 water glasses or glass jars of equal size
- ☐ 2 water pitchers
- ☐ bag of crushed ice and a cooler to store it in
- ☐ paper bowls
- ☐ serving spoons
- ☐ butter knife
- ☐ plastic spoons
- ☐ pan of red gelatin, cubed, or gelatin cups*
- ☐ green gummy frogs (or green gummy worms cut in pieces)*
- ☐ sweet grape powdered soft drink mix*
- ☐ raisins*
- ☐ animal crackers*
- ☐ Red Hots cinnamon candies*
- ☐ crunchy corn puff cereal*
- ☐ masking tape
- ☐ photocopies of the "Be Strong in the Lord Bracelets" handout (p. 43)
- ☐ scissors

* Always check for allergies before serving snacks.

LESSON AIM

To help kids understand that ★ *God is bigger and more powerful than anyone.*

OBJECTIVES

Kids will

- ✓ experience trying to help another group, but will ruin that group's efforts instead,
- ✓ participate in an interactive Bible story about Moses confronting Pharaoh,
- ✓ play a game in which God's people are protected, and
- ✓ make a take-home reminder to be strong in God's mighty power.

BIBLE BASIS

 Exodus 7:10–10:20

You've got to feel for Moses during the first part of this passage. He and Aaron win the Israelites over. They get their courage up, and in concert with the Israelite elders, approach Pharaoh's throne to take on the meanest, most powerful monarch in the world, only to be scoffed out of the palace. Can you just hear the "neener-neener" in Pharaoh's voice? "Who is the Lord that *I* should obey him? I do not know the Lord and I will *not* let them go!"

To further show what a nice guy he was, Pharaoh put a

All Together Now

terrible burden on the Israelites' already overwhelming workload. Up to this point the Israelite slaves had been provided straw to make their bricks. As punishment for Moses' impertinence, they not only had to maintain their brick quotas, but also scrounge for their own straw. When the Israelites couldn't keep up, Pharaoh's soldiers beat their foremen. Pharaoh accused them of being lazy.

Collectively the Israelite leaders said to Moses, "Thanks a lot. Now look what you've done! We were better off before you came!"

What a letdown for the former prince, who was reluctant to accept this job in the first place. I don't know about you, but I would've run all the way back to Midian. But, as is usually the case, God's work is not about the comfort of the individuals involved—it's about making an unforgettable statement to the world. So Moses went back over and over again, and before the entire process of the plagues was over, his own people and the nobles of Egypt held him in high regard.

Moses' work wasn't about himself. He was representing the living God, the great I AM. Pharaoh had yet to meet the God of Israel, but, oh boy, was he about to. This proud, hard-hearted ruler assumed that because of his vast holdings, wealth, and mighty armies, there was no conflict he couldn't win. Wrong!

At first, Egyptian magicians were able to reproduce the plagues God sent in some form or another. But before long they found themselves unable to keep up with—or even survive—the displays of power put on by almighty God. (Interestingly, swarms of locusts still create devastating loss across the world today. You'll find a fascinating article about their transformation from harmless, shy creatures of the desert to the nefarious hordes that God unleashed through Moses at http://earthobservatory.nasa.gov/features/locusts.)

As Pharaoh became more desperate, he began to offer deals to Moses: Sacrifice to your God but do it here in Egypt; go sacrifice to your God but leave your flocks here. God wasn't interested in bargaining with Pharaoh. But even when his people and highest advisers must have been begging the proud Pharaoh to let the Israelites go, Pharaoh's pride wouldn't bend until his heart was broken—but that's a story for the next lesson.

📖 Ephesians 6:10

Willingly or not, Moses was God's champion in a great duel with Pharaoh. God had given Moses a sidekick in his brother Aaron. However, one senses that Moses would've been happier quietly tending sheep than firing God's devastating salvos in this cosmic duel. After all, as author Chuck Swindoll amusingly puts it, he was the "Here am I, send Aaron" guy.

Before every bout with Pharaoh and his magicians, Moses drew his strength from God and his mighty power. Do you suppose Moses had any idea that after God dealt the awful, winning blow, he would also stretch Moses' job into a 40-year assignment?

UNDERSTANDING YOUR KIDS

Have you noticed kids' enduring affection for superheroes? The many incarnations of the Man of Steel? The Transformers, who just keep getting bigger and badder? Men who morph into bat and spider guys? Imagine the lively discussion that would ensue if you asked, "Which movie or TV superhero would you like to be—and why?"

It's no wonder kids love these stronger-than-human, save-the-day types. The world is a downright scary place. Instant access to news means instant access to catastrophe after disaster after war. Halfway around the globe is suddenly next door. Oh, how kids would love to have a little of that BAM! SHAZAM! stuff of their very own.

Use this lesson to teach kids that the power of God is greater by far than any other power—real or imagined.

All Together Now

ATTENTION GRABBER

You Ruined Everything!

Before class, set out seven water glasses or glass jars of equal size beside a sink. To create musical tones, fill one of them completely. Tap it with a butter knife. This will be your lowest note, or the word *me* in the lyrics for the song "Jesus Loves Me." Using that glass as a guide, fill three other glasses appropriately to find the notes for *Je-sus* and *loves*. Leave three glasses empty for the phrase *this I know*. If you don't have a sink, transport the glasses and pitchers of water to your room. Cover the water experiment to hide it. You'll need an assistant to work with one of the groups—a musical person if you're not, or a person who'll lead Group 2 on a long treasure hunt for a bag of ice. Hide a well-wrapped bag of ice chips inside a cooler in an unlikely place in your church or in the immediate area. It might even be in the trunk of your car.

Say: **Welcome! I have a couple of challenges today and I think you're going to love them. Before we begin, let's form two groups. For these challenges I'm going to hand pick your groups.**

For Group 1, choose kids who are musical and who enjoy a challenge. For Group 2, choose kids who need to move those muscles and get the kinks out. As you're forming groups, don't say anything about why you're putting certain kids into either group. Just explain that it's going to be a mystery for now.

Once your groups are chosen, separate them. Their individual group leaders will explain their challenges separately.

GROUP 1

Place the glasses, the pitchers, and a butter knife in the center of a table. Arrange four glasses in order so you can play the tones for the first four notes of "Jesus Loves Me."

Say: **Learning what you can from the way these water glasses are filled, it's your job to fill the last three glasses so they create the musical tones for the phrase *this I know*. Here's a tip: The more water you put in a glass, the lower the tone will be; the less water you put in a glass, the higher the tone will be.**

Demonstrate by tapping the lowest and highest tones of the glasses you've already "tuned." Let kids experiment by pouring water from a pitcher into a cup, and then pouring some back if the tone is too low or adding water if it's too high. Don't demand pitch-perfect tones—something close will be fine. Cheer kids on in their efforts, and let them do most of the work.

GROUP 2

Take these kids into the hall and out of earshot of Group 1. You'll be looking for the well-wrapped bag of ice chips hidden prior to class.

Say: **We've been given a tough secret mission. We've got to find a secret treasure hidden somewhere in or around our church. All I can tell you is this: It's in a bag about the size of a grocery bag.**

Let several kids guess the bag's whereabouts; follow up on all their suggestions at a slow run, but remind the kids that it's a secret mission so they'll have to run quietly enough not to disturb anyone else in church. Time your quest. When five minutes is about up, suggest the actual location of the bag.

Say: **Hey—what if we look in the** [name of location]**?**

Once you've found the bag of ice, open it and let everybody nibble some. Then suggest: **You know, I bet the kids in Group 1 have been working as hard as we have.**

Ask:

• Tell why you think we should—or shouldn't—go back and share some of our treasure with them.

When you run back to the room, burst in with great enthusiasm. Don't give the Group 1 kids time to tell you about what they've been doing. Instead, say: **Hey, we've had to work really hard on our quest for secret treasure. You look like you've been working hard, too, so we'd like to share our treasure with you!**

Before anyone can say a word, plop some ice into the glasses on the table and encourage your kids to do the same. Wait for the kids in Group 1 to wail, "Oh, no!"

Look shocked and say: **But you seemed to be working so hard! All we wanted to do was share a little ice water with you. What's wrong?**

Let Group 1 kids explain what they were doing. Then cover your mouth with your hand and say: **Oops!**

Before anyone feels too bad, explain that this experience was no accident. Say: **Both leaders knew what the other group was doing and what would happen in the end.**

Ask:

• Group 1 kids, how did it feel for your efforts to be disrupted by the Group 2 kids?

• Group 2 kids, how did you feel once you realized you may've hurt the hard work done by the Group 1 kids?

• Everyone, tell about a time you've experienced your hard work getting "messed up" by someone else.

All Together Now

We let this happen so you'd feel how Moses and the Israelites felt the first time Moses went to Pharaoh. It was kind of like our unfortunate event here—only much worse. The Israelites were angry and Moses felt terrible! But he learned that ★ *God is bigger and more powerful than anyone!* Now let's get right into the Bible story.

BIBLE EXPLORATION

. . . .

Plague Soup (Exodus 7:10–10:20)

Before class, place the food supplies (used for Plague Soup) in a box or other container. You'll want to take out the ingredients one at a time so that kids aren't distracted by seeing all of them at once.

Say: **The Israelites had been slaves in Egypt for more than 400 years. So Moses and Aaron went to Pharaoh and said, "God says, 'Let my people, the Israelites, go into the wilderness and worship me.' "**

Say this after me: Let my people go! Pause for kids to repeat. **But Pharaoh just laughed at Moses. "I don't even know your God, and I'm not letting the Israelites go," he answered. And that was that. Then Pharaoh told the slave masters to order the Israelite slaves to make the same number of bricks, but now the slaves would have to find the straw they needed themselves.**

Say this after me: No straw! Make bricks! Pause for kids to repeat.

There was no way the Israelites could make as many bricks without straw. Some of the other Israelite leaders went to Pharaoh and begged him to change his mind, but Pharaoh just told them to get back to work—without any straw.

Say this after me again: No straw! Make bricks! Pause for kids to repeat.

It looked like Moses had messed up everything. The Israelites were furious with Moses. They knew he meant to help, but he'd just made everything worse. Moses cried out to God for help. And God heard. Pharaoh may not have known who God was—but he was just about to find out.

Let's move to a table now, because for the rest of our story, we're going to make Plague Soup!

Give every child a paper bowl.

Teacher Tip

This lesson deals with the first eight plagues. The next lesson covers the two remaining plagues.

Say: **Once more, Moses went before Pharaoh and said, "Let my people go!" But Pharaoh ignored him. So soon after, Aaron raised his staff over the Nile River and all the water turned to blood. All the water in containers turned to blood, too. The people couldn't find anything to drink.**

The first ingredient in our Plague Soup will be red gelatin to represent the blood-red Nile River.

Give each child a scoop of cubed, red gelatin.

Say: **After a week, God told Moses to go back to Pharaoh and say, "Unless you let my people go, I will send a plague of frogs over your land. They'll come up out of the river into your pots and pans and even into your beds. There will be frogs everywhere you look!" But Pharaoh wouldn't let the people go. So Aaron raised the staff and soon frogs filled every room in the palace and every house in Egypt. The second ingredient in our Plague Soup will be gummy frogs (or pieces of green gummy worms) to represent the plague of frogs.**

Sprinkle gummy frogs (or green gummy worm pieces) into each child's bowl.

Say: **Soon Pharaoh called to Moses and begged him to make the frogs go away. He promised to let the Israelites go. So Moses prayed and the frogs went away. But as soon as they were gone, Pharaoh changed his mind and decided to keep his slaves.**

Then Moses went to Pharaoh and said, "Let God's people go or God will send a plague of gnats."

Say this after me: Let my people go! Pause for kids to repeat. **Aaron raised the staff and swarms of little gnats covered Egypt. They covered all the people and animals. Eeeww! The third ingredient in our Plague Soup will be powdered grape drink mix. Its little grains are tiny and gritty like little gnats.**

Sprinkle grape powdered drink mix in each bowl.

Say: **The next day, Moses said to Pharaoh, "God says to let his people go or he will send flies to cover your land. But this time God will protect his own people—there will be no flies in the land of Goshen, where they live."**

Say this after me: Let my people go! Pause for kids to repeat.

God did just as he had said. Thick layers of flies filled the palace and all of Egypt. But there were no flies in the land of Goshen, where the Israelites lived.

All Together Now

The fourth ingredient in our Plague Soup will be raisins to represent flies.

Sprinkle raisins in each child's bowl.

Say: **Before too long Pharaoh called for Moses. "All right, go ahead and worship your God," he said. "But do it right here in this land."**

"No!" Moses replied. "We must go into the wilderness as God commands."

"All right!" Pharaoh said. "I'll let you go tomorrow. Just make these flies go away."

But once the flies were gone, Pharaoh changed his mind once again and refused to let God's people go. Moses went to Pharaoh *again!*

Say this after me: Let my people go! Pause for kids to repeat. **Moses said, "God says if you don't let his people go to worship him, a plague will strike your cattle and sheep. But none of the cattle and sheep in the land of Goshen will die."**

Pharaoh ignored Moses. But, sure enough, the next morning the cattle and sheep that belonged to the Egyptians got sick and died. The animals in the land of Goshen stayed strong and healthy. But did Pharaoh let God's people go? No!

The fifth ingredient in our Plague Soup will be animal crackers!

Give children each a few animal crackers.

Say: **Because Pharaoh wouldn't listen to God, the next plague was painful sores that broke out on all the Egyptians, including Pharaoh and his officials.**

Did you ever have a big, red sore that lasted for days and days, like maybe from a spider bite?

That's what happened to all the Egyptians, but it was even worse. Still Pharaoh would not let God's people go.

The sixth ingredient in our Plague Soup will be cinnamon candies to represent the painful sores.

Sprinkle a few Red Hots candies in each child's bowl.

Say: **Moses warned Pharaoh that God would send a terrible hailstorm next. When the hail began to pound to the ground, all the trees were stripped, the crops were ruined, and animals left outside were killed. Thunder and hail and lightning roared on and on, tearing up everything! But there was no storm in the land of Goshen.**

The seventh ingredient in our Plague Soup will be a blast of ice chips for hail.

Dash a large spoonful of ice chips over each child's Plague Soup.

Say: **Pharaoh called Moses to the palace right away. "I have sinned!" Pharaoh said. "Please make this terrible storm stop and I'll let God's people go." Moses prayed and God stopped the storm.**

Do you think Pharaoh let God's people go?

He didn't! As soon as the storm was over, his heart became hard and he decided to keep his slaves. Oh, Pharaoh, what's it going to take?

God sent Moses to Pharaoh one more time. Moses said, "God says to let his people go or he will send swarms of locusts over the land that will devour everything in their path."

Say this after me: Let my people go! Pause for kids to repeat. **Pharaoh was a proud man. He wouldn't back down. So the next day swarms of locusts appeared like great clouds. They landed on the grass and the crops and the trees and ate them. They stripped the land bare. Pharaoh called for Moses and begged him to make the locusts go away. Like before, Pharaoh promised to let the Israelites go. And, like before, as soon as the locusts were gone, Pharaoh changed his mind.**

The last ingredient in our Plague Soup is cereal to represent the locusts. Sprinkle a bit of puffed corn cereal on each child's Plague Soup. Then hand out spoons and invite kids to dig in as you digest the story.

Let's eat our Plague Soup.

As kids eat, ask:

• When God sent all these plagues on Egypt, why do you think Pharaoh didn't let God's people go?

• Describe the plague you think was the worst so far, and why.

• What do you think about the plagues God sent?

LIFE APPLICATION
. . . .
No Plagues on Me

Use masking tape to divide your play area into three equal spaces. Have kids scatter across the spaces.

Say: **The space on this side** (point left) **is called Goshen, the land where God's people lived. God protected his people from the plagues. The space in the center is called the Nile,**

All Together Now

the great river of Egypt. The space on the other side (point right) **is Egypt, where God sent his worst plagues.**

If I call out "Goshen," everyone runs for Goshen. If I call out "the Nile," everyone runs for the Nile. I could also call out, "Take a dive!" Then everyone does a belly flop in the Nile. Finally, if I call out "Egypt," everyone runs for Egypt. Let's practice.

Call out a few commands to get kids into the game.

Then say: **Now I might get a little tricky in my calls. For instance, I might call "Goshen" but point to Egypt. Or I might point in two directions at once. Or I might call names really fast to confuse you. Anytime you cross the wrong line, you're out. We'll see who lasts the longest!**

Make your last call Goshen, and then call "End game! Freeze!" before everyone has time to get to Goshen.

Say: **Drop in place.**

Ask:

• **Why do you think God protected the people of Goshen?**

Say: **Everyone who is *not* in Goshen, form a strong wall around those who are. I'm going to be a nasty plague trying to break through. Your job is to scrunch together so I can't get through. Ready?**

Make a nasty "plague face" as you push against your kids with medium force, but not enough force to overcome their wall. Try two or three times; then shake your head and say: **You've got me beat.**

One reason God protected his people in Goshen is so they'd learn to be strong in the Lord. In other words, they'd learn that ★ *God is bigger and more powerful than anyone.* Let's make some cool bracelets to remind us of that.

Teacher Tip

If kids are easily confused at first, don't hesitate to start new rounds of the game. As the kids get better, call out the places at a rapid-fire pace.

COMMITMENT

Be Strong in the Lord Bracelets

Distribute copies of the "Be Strong in the Lord Bracelets" handouts and scissors. Show kids how to cut out the bracelet strips and then fold the side pieces toward the middle on the dotted lines. Have them make the edges of the folds sharp using their fingernails or the edge of scissors.

Have kids continue to pinch the edges of the fold, curling the edges of the bracelet toward the inside. You may need to help younger kids get a good curl to their bracelets before proceeding.

Have everyone watch as you carefully slip the blank end of the bracelet into the folded pocket of the printed end. By gently coaxing, you can continue to slip the blank end in until *The Lord* meets *Be Strong*. The "fold hold" is quite secure. Let kids size their bracelets to fit their wrists.

CLOSING

Arm Yourselves!

Gather kids in a circle.

Say: **Now that we've made these great bracelets, let's arm ourselves together! When I say, "Be strong in the Lord," slide your bracelet on and hold your arm up in the air.**

Be strong in the Lord!

Good job! Now raise your other arm and hold hands with the person next to you. I'll close in prayer.

Pray: **Dear God, you are the one who made the universe, who made us, and who protected your people from the terrible plagues you sent on Egypt. Help us always remember that ★** *you are bigger and more powerful than anyone.* **Amen!**

Be Strong in the Lord Bracelets

God used his mighty power to send terrible plagues on Egypt, but he protected his people in Goshen. Wear this cool bracelet as your very own reminder that ★ *God is bigger and more powerful than anyone.*

1. Cut out the bracelet on the heavy solid line.
2. Fold the side pieces back on the dotted lines.

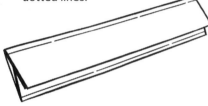

3. Pinch the folds, curling them toward the inside.

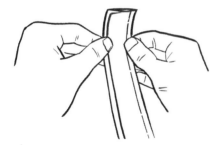

4. Slip the blank end of the bracelet into the folded pocket of the printed end. Make it just the size you need.

BE STRONG IN THE LORD

Published in *All Together Now, Volume 1* by Group Publishing, Inc., 1515 Cascade Ave., Loveland, CO 80538.

The God of Light and Life

You'll need...

- [ ] blankets
- [ ] heavy-duty black garbage bags you've cut open
- [ ] wide painter's tape
- [ ] scissors
- [ ] small flashlight
- [ ] photocopies of the "Israelite House" handout (p. 49)
- [ ] glue sticks
- [ ] red markers
- [ ] photocopies of the "House Base" handout (p. 52) on heavy paper
- [ ] cellophane tape
- [ ] paper cutter

LESSON AIM

To help kids believe that ★ *God takes care of us.*

OBJECTIVES

Kids will

✓ use materials to create the darkest spot possible,

✓ participate in an interactive story of the plague of darkness and the Passover,

✓ create a small Israelite village, and

✓ celebrate Jesus' light.

BIBLE BASIS

 **Exodus 10:21–12:50**

Pharaoh the Stubborn and Proud wouldn't be bent by all the plagues God sent that were ruining Egypt. Though his advisers were begging him to let Moses take the Hebrews and go, Pharaoh would have none of it. Who was this God of the Hebrews to challenge Pharaoh, ruler of all Egypt, Pharaoh of the darkened heart?

We almost get the feeling that God had been toying with Pharaoh up to this point, so that this duel of wills, this battle for the title of Supremely Powerful, would become such an epic that it would be told for centuries. For in one fell swoop, God crushes Pharaoh's will and has all of Egypt praising Moses and gifting the Hebrews with its wealth as God's people follow

Moses' directions for a hasty departure.

The prelude to the final plague of the death of the firstborn was three days' darkness—a thick, tangible darkness in which the Egyptians could neither see each other nor leave their own dwellings. How fitting a warning for people who worshipped the sun god, Ra. After all, God is the author of light. Pharaoh's ultimate rejection of God resulted in the complete loss of light and spoke into that fear of the unknown: *If Moses' God can do this, is there anything he can't do? What kind of fool is Pharaoh not to heed this warning and obey the commands of such a God?*

So we hear Moses' careful instructions to the Hebrews about preparing for the Passover—painting the blood of a spotless lamb on the lintels and door posts of their homes—and we see straight forward to the cross of Jesus Christ, where he poured his blood on a cross to lead all of us from the darkness of sin into the freedom of his glorious light.

Thanks be to God.

 **1 John 1:5, 7**

Everything about the Passover points directly to the path of salvation God had planned through Jesus. To be saved, the Hebrews painted the blood of a spotless lamb on the lintels and door posts of their homes. We're saved by our belief in Jesus Christ and his sacrificial death and resurrection on our behalf. We're not isolated individuals without a past or a future. Instead, we're a faraway people drawn near, strangers adopted into the family of Abraham by faith. And so we live in the glorious light of the living Word who was there when the words "let there be light" (Genesis 1:3) burst across a dawning universe. In the darkest hours of our lives, ★ *God takes care of us.*

UNDERSTANDING YOUR KIDS

Can you remember being afraid of the dark as a child? The curtains that were friendly the moment before the light went off suddenly cast looming shadows; the open closet door yawned into a chasm of unknown frights.

With maturity, these childish fears fade, yet the fear of the unknown remains. Use the dramatic symbolism of darkness and light in this lesson to challenge your kids to live in the light that Jesus offers.

THE LESSON »

ATTENTION GRABBER

Here in the Dark

Ask:

• **Describe how you feel about being in the dark.**

• **What is it about the dark that makes you feel that way?**

Say: **Sometimes the dark brings with it the mystery of the unknown. For instance, at home we know just when to step around a chair or turn down a hallway. But in other houses or buildings we don't know so well, we don't know what to expect, so the dark is a little scarier.**

Ask:

• **Tell about the darkest dark you've ever been in.**

Say: **Usually when we talk about "the dark," there's light from a streetlight or from the stars or a night light in the bathroom. If you've ever been in an underground cave, you know that's a different kind of darkness. The darkness is so dark you can't even see your hand when you hold it right up in front of your face.**

Let's do a little experiment. Working together, let's see how dark you can make one little area of our room. The area needs to fit everyone. I have these materials for you to use.

Set out blankets, black garbage bags that you've cut open, wide painter's tape, and scissors. Add other materials as you like. Tell kids not to put the plastic near their face or anyone else's. Monitor kids carefully while they work with the materials.

Say: **I'd love to see how you work together on this project without my help. Choose a Crew Chief whose job is to listen to everyone's ideas. I'll give you two minutes to talk over your ideas and then report back to me.**

Call time after two minutes, and ask the Crew Chief to share the ideas. Ask kids which idea they like best. If possible, let kids carry out their favorite idea.

Say: **Let's get to work! Crew Chief, it's your job to ensure everyone has a part in our construction project.**

Let the kids' chosen Crew Chief direct the work. As the kids work, continue to monitor their safe use of black plastic.

Once the dark area is completed, dim the room lights, grab your flashlight, and lead the kids into the darkened area they've created.

Teacher Tip

Be careful to guide the discussion so kids who admit to feeling uncomfortable in the dark aren't perceived as being "chicken." You might explain that you feel okay in the dark in your own home, but not in unfamiliar places.

Teacher Tip

If you have more than eight kids, you might want to form two crews with an additional leader for this activity.

Teacher Tip

Giving kids choices creates ownership of what's going on in the class and goes a long way toward wiping out discipline problems.

All Together Now

BIBLE EXPLORATION

. . . .

Pharaoh, Pharaoh! (Exodus 10:21–12:50)

Once the kids are settled in your darkened area, ask:

• **How would you describe how dark your special area turned out to be?**

Say: **Last week, we learned about eight plagues that happened in Egypt, but there were actually ten. Pharaoh wouldn't let the Israelites go.**

Have kids say, "Boo, Pharaoh, boo!"

So God had two more plagues in store for the very hard-hearted Pharaoh. The first one was the plague of darkness. The darkness God sent on Egypt was no ordinary darkness. The Bible tells us it was darkness so thick you could *feel* it.

Have kids say, "Wow, now that's dark!"

It says that the Egyptians couldn't see each other and that they didn't leave their homes. And, of course, they didn't know how long this darkness would go on.

Finally, after three days of darkness, Pharaoh called Moses. "You can take your people and worship your God," he said, **"but you must leave your animals and flocks here."**

Have kids say, "Boo, Pharaoh, boo!"

"Our flocks and animals must go with us so we will have sacrifices to make to our God," Moses answered.

Pharaoh was furious!

"Get out of my sight!" he told Moses. "I never want to see your face again."

Have kids say, "Boo, Pharaoh, boo!"

Because Pharaoh disobeyed God, a plague much worse than all the others was about to befall Egypt. Moses hurried to tell God's people, the Israelites, what to do. Let's hurry out of here.

Lead kids out of your darkened area into the storytelling area of your room.

Moses had already warned Pharaoh that the last plague would be the worst of all, but Pharaoh didn't pay any attention. For the last plague, God would cause all the firstborn sons of Egypt to die, right about midnight on a certain night. That included even Pharaoh's firstborn son, but not the firstborn sons of God's people, Israel.

Have kids say, "Pharaoh, you should've listened!"

Here's why God's people would be spared from this

terrible plague: God gave them special instructions that they would have to follow exactly.

First, they had to choose a perfect 1-year-old lamb or goat and give him special treatment for four days. Then they must kill the lamb and get him ready to eat. They had to take a little of the lamb's blood and smear it on the top and sides of their doors. The blood on their doors would show that they were God's people and were following his special instructions.

Let's create a small Israelite village to see how this worked.

Lead kids to a craft table. Set out copies of the "Israelite House" handout, scissors, and glue sticks. Show kids how to create a 3-D Israelite House by cutting out the house, folding back the sides and the tabs, rubbing glue sticks on the tabs, and sticking the house together. Also, cut open *one* side and the top of the door so it opens.

Once kids have assembled their houses, gather the group together in a circle.

Say: **Now let's put the houses together to form a village. God's people lived together in an area called Goshen. None of the terrible things that happened to the Egyptians happened to God's people in Goshen because ★** *God takes care of us.*

For our little village, let's use red markers to represent the lamb's blood. You just need a little on the top and the sides of the door.

Pass red markers around as you continue. Keep an eye on kids' work so they add just a bit of red marker around the doors of their houses. Also have them add their initials on the back of the houses. Then collect the markers and set them out of sight.

Say: **After midnight, nobody could go outside, for God would pass through Egypt and all the firstborn sons would be killed. But anyone who had the special mark of blood on the door would be safe.**

And that's just what happened. A little after midnight God's people could hear terrible wailing and crying all through Egypt where the firstborn sons had died. But all the firstborn sons of the Israelites were safe, because families had put the blood of the lamb on their doors.

After this, Pharaoh called Moses and said, "Take your people and go!"

You see, in the middle of this dark, dark night, Pharaoh finally realized that he couldn't win a contest against God.

Have kids say, "Pharaoh, you should have listened!"

Teacher Tip

You'll want to finish the Israelite houses fairly quickly to get back to the Bible story. It's a very simple craft. If you have several younger kids, you may want to pre-cut their houses or have assistants or older kids help them.

All Together Now

Israelite House

When God sent the last terrible plague through Egypt, he "passed over" the Israelite houses that had the blood of a lamb painted on the top and sides of the doors.

1. Add a bit of red to the door with marker, and then cut out your house.
2. Fold down the walls, fold back the tabs, and rub a glue stick on them to hold the house together.
3. Make the door open by cutting one side and the top of the door.

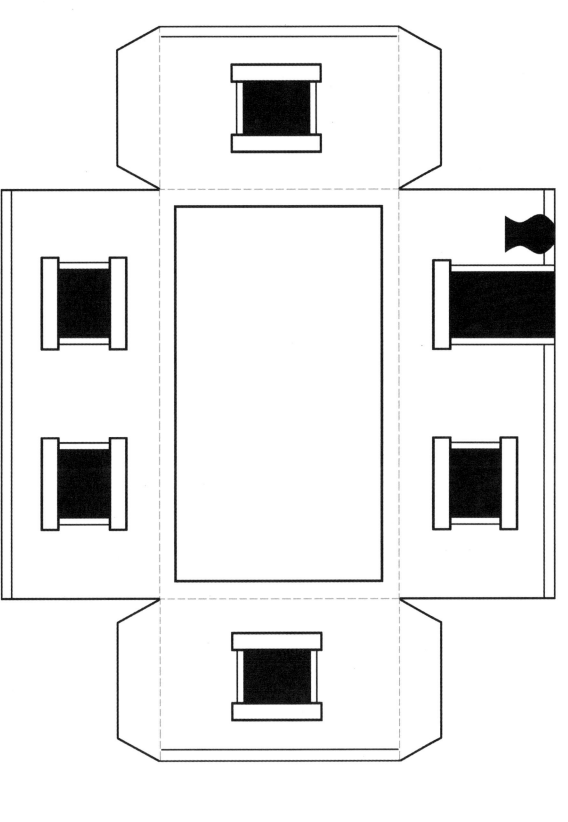

· ·

Jesus, Our Sacrifice

Say: **Now follow me back to the dark spot we created, and I'll tell you some very surprising news!**

Take your flashlight and a copy of the "House Base" handout. When everyone is settled in the darkened area, turn on the flashlight.

Say: **People who trust in Jesus never have to go through a dark night like the Egyptians did. Listen to these words from 1 John in the Bible:**

This is the message we heard from Jesus and now declare to you: God is light, and there is no darkness in him at all...But if we are living in the light, as God is in the light, then we have fellowship with each other, and the blood of Jesus, his Son, cleanses us from all sin. (1 John 1:5, 7)

Ask:

• **What do these verses say about how Jesus takes care of us?**

• **How is Jesus' blood like the blood of the lamb on the Israelites' door posts?**

Say: **Many of the things that happened in the Old Testament point straight to things that later happened with Jesus in the New Testament. I'll explain just a couple of them here. Jesus was called "the Lamb of God who takes away the sin of the world."**

The Israelites killed a lamb so they wouldn't die. When Jesus died on the cross, he made a way for us to never die.

Say: **We don't need to sacrifice animals anymore, because Jesus became the sacrifice for all our sins, for all time. That's why we call him ★ *our Savior, who takes care of us.***

This is a wonderful time to present an invitation for your kids to put their trust in Jesus.

Say: **Since people who believe in Jesus live in the light of God, let's go out into the light from our dark place!**

COMMITMENT

. . . .

Jesus, Our Light

Gather kids around the craft table. Before class, use a paper cutter to cut the "House Base" handouts into half sheets. Set out copies of the "House Base" handouts and cellophane tape.

You'll see this handout has a special place to tape on the Israelite house you made earlier. It also contains the verse I read a moment ago:

This is the message we heard from Jesus and now declare to you: God is light, and there is no darkness in him at all...But if we are living in the light, as God is in the light, then we have fellowship with each other, and the blood of Jesus, his Son, cleanses us from all sin. (1 John 1:5, 7)

Tape your house onto the handout.

Say: **Let's read these wonderful verses from 1 John together. If you're older, find a younger friend to read with. Follow along with the group.**

Lead the kids in reading the verses from the handout.

Say: **As a way to thank God for Jesus, give high fives to everyone around you, but be careful not to smash your cool houses!**

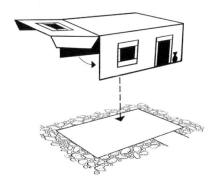

Teacher Tip

There's no cutting with this handout. Kids simply tape their houses to the indicated spot.

CLOSING

. . . .

Jesus, Always With Us

Say: **Place your houses carefully on the floor behind you. Then make a tight, shoulder-to-shoulder circle. Let's pray.**

Dear Jesus, thank you for being our light. Thank you for ★*taking care of us.* **Help us to trust you more every day. In your name we pray. Amen!**

House Base

"This is the message we heard from Jesus and now declare to you: God is light and in him there is no darkness at all...But if we are living in the light, as God is in the light, then we have fellowship with each other, and the blood of Jesus, his Son, cleanses us from all sin." (1 John 1:5, 7)

House Base

"This is the message we heard from Jesus and now declare to you: God is light and in him there is no darkness at all...But if we are living in the light, as God is in the light, then we have fellowship with each other, and the blood of Jesus, his Son, cleanses us from all sin." (1 John 1:5, 7)

Standoff at the Red Sea

LESSON AIM

To help kids see that no matter how terrifying the challenge, ★*God helps us when we're in trouble.*

OBJECTIVES

Kids will

✓ be challenged to stand still no matter what happens,

✓ participate in an interactive story of the face-off of Pharaoh and the Israelites at the Red Sea,

✓ make a 3-D Red Sea reminder that God will help them when they're in trouble,

✓ share times they've patiently waited for God's help, and

✓ pray that God will lead them through tough challenges in their lives.

BIBLE BASIS

 **Exodus 13:17—15:21**

It came down to this. After 430 years, the Israelites were free from Egyptian oppression. After the plague of the death of the firstborn, nearly 2 million of God's people left the land of Goshen in the middle of the night and headed for Succoth. From there, God led them on a circuitous route with a pillar of cloud by day and a pillar of fire by night. When it dawned on Pharaoh that he'd let his huge workforce go, a huge snarl twisted his face; then he assembled his army, called for his

You'll need...

☐ kitchen timer

☐ lifelike baby doll

☐ cooking pans

☐ scarf

☐ old blanket

☐ shiny blue fabric, blue bedsheets, or blue vinyl party tablecloths

☐ 2 classroom tables

☐ junior high or high school volunteers

☐ photocopies of the "God Helps Us When We're in Trouble" handout (p. 61)

☐ scissors

☐ glue sticks

☐ pencils

☐ gummy bears*

☐ baskets of artificial ferns and other greenery *(optional)*

* Always check for allergies before serving snacks.

chariot, and set out after them. And they met in a location that left the Israelites tactically helpless, backed up against the Red Sea.

As the Israelites sweated out their predicament in the face of Pharaoh's approaching chariots, they quickly turned on Moses. "We told you to leave us alone and let us serve the Egyptians. Weren't there enough graves in Egypt that we had to come to die here in the desert?" From our perspective it seems like they had awfully short memories regarding all God had done for them in Egypt. But then, who wants to face down a charging army?

Don't you just love God's instructions? "Don't be afraid. Just stand still and watch the Lord rescue you today. The Egyptians you see today will never be seen again. The Lord himself will fight for you. Just stay calm" (Exodus 14:13-14). Stand still? Wouldn't you have been inclined to at least pick up a stick?

Ah, the wonder and mystery of God. Moses did pick up a stick—his staff—and God parted the sea so the Israelites could walk through on dry ground. When they were safely through, Moses stretched out his staff again, causing the walls of water to collapse on the pursuing Egyptians.

📖 Psalm 46:10

Throughout the drama of the first chapters of Exodus until the night of the Passover preparations, God asked nothing of his people except to be still. They were still as they watched plague after plague befall Pharaoh and the Egyptians. And now, as they faced what would seem to be imminent destruction by the Egyptians, God asked them again to be still.

Being still can be the hardest thing God ever asks us to do. We tend to want to fix every situation. But sometimes God just wants us to leave things to him. Then when he finally does say "go!" it's up to us to lace up those hiking boots and cross while the ground is dry.

UNDERSTANDING YOUR KIDS

Precious and few are the kids who have any "wait" in them. The ability to wait until God says "go" comes with years of maturity. On the other hand, children never cease to amaze us with their ability to comprehend, retain, and act on the deepest of spiritual concepts when those concepts are presented in ways they can understand. Use this lesson to introduce kids to the concept that sometimes God wants us to wait until ★ *he helps us when we're in trouble.*

All Together Now

....

Be Still!

Say: **I have a very unusual challenge for you today. In fact, I'm quite sure some of you have never faced a challenge like this before. It's simply this: Once we begin our game, you must stand still. Don't move a muscle—not a wiggle, not a twitch. No matter what I do or say, you must remain perfectly still. Think you're up for a challenge like that?**

Okay, let's get started. First of all, stand in a circle, a nice arm's length apart. I'm going to set this timer for three minutes. Once it starts ticking, you need to be as frozen as an iceberg. No exceptions. I will try to fool you, but don't buy it. Got it? Here we go.

Set the timer, and then say: **Oh, I forgot to put this in the middle of the circle. Let me through right here, would you?**

If kids move to let you through, have them sit down away from the circle—they're out of the game.

Use these various tricks to get your kids to move.

• Say "hi" to various kids. If they say anything, they're out of the game.

• Clap your hands loudly behind someone.

• Say, "Oh, I see a little dirt here," fold down that person's ear, and tickle behind it.

• Yell, "Boo!" behind someone.

• Say: "Okay, that's enough. Everyone sit down." *(Actually, you're not done.)*

Each time a person moves, have him or her sit down away from the circle.

After the timer goes off, congratulate the kids who are still standing. Then gather everyone for discussion.

Ask:

• **Why did some of you move when I told you to stand still?**

• **Tell about other times it's hard to stand still.**

Say: **Today we're going to hear about the greatest challenge that faced the Israelites after they escaped from Egypt. Strangely enough, God gave them these directions: Be still and I will fight for you. That may sound easy, but as in our game, it wasn't at all easy for the Israelites to do with what they were facing. Let's plunge into our Bible story and find out how ★ *God helped them when they were in trouble.***

BIBLE EXPLORATION

. . . .

Horse and Rider (Exodus 13:17—15:21)

Before class, decide on a destination within your church where you'll lead your caravan. Also arrange for a class of junior high or high school kids to act as Pharaoh's attacking army. This is a great little "missions project" for the visiting class.

Say: **God had just sent 10 plagues on Pharaoh and the country of Egypt. Finally, Pharaoh had had enough and told the Israelites to leave.**

In the middle of the night, God sent a message to Moses to take all the Israelites and get out of town! The Israelites had carefully followed Moses' instructions to be ready, so soon they marched out of Egypt—nearly 2 million of them! God appeared to them in a big cloud of fire and led them into the wilderness to a camping site.

Can you imagine what that journey out of Egypt in the middle of the night must've been like? The Israelites had been slaves in Egypt for 430 years. That's longer than the lifetimes of four people together—if they each live to be more than 100! Mothers had to carry children too young to walk. They probably had carts for people who were too old to walk. They took clothes and a few cooking pots. They took their sheep and goats and cattle. And nearly 2 million people! Let's see if we can recreate the scene.

Ask:

• Who wants to be an older person who needs help walking? How will we help this person?

Show an old blanket and suggest moving your "senior citizen" on the blanket.

• Who'll volunteer to help move our senior citizen?

• Who wants be a mother carrying a young child and some pots and pans?

Hand this child a lifelike doll along with some cooking pans wrapped in a scarf to sling over one shoulder.

• Who wants to be a sheep? a goat? a cow? a shepherd who'll move them along?

• Who wants to be the father who'll watch over this family?

Make sure each child has a part.

Say: **Now, we're ready to escape from Egypt. I'll be Moses. Let's go!**

Lead your caravan to the destination within your church that you decided upon prior to class, and then lead kids back to your room.

Say: **Good job, everyone!**

Ask:

• **What did you discover during our caravan experience?**

• **What would it be like to be part of a caravan of almost 2 million people—leaving in the middle of the night?**

Say: **Wow! That must've been kind of crazy, huh? Especially for hard-working slaves who'd never done anything except what their masters told them to do. Suddenly they were free and on their own. It was a good thing God was there to guide them!**

God had them wander around for a couple of days, but the reason was a big secret. If you lean in close, I'll tell you.

Create an air of excitement as you say in a stage whisper: **God wasn't quite done with Pharaoh yet! Ooooh, no! You see, after a couple of days, Pharaoh started thinking, "What have I done? I've let all my slaves go! Now who'll do all the work?"**

Then he got an evil look on his face, rubbed his hands together, and told his leaders, "We're going after them!" Uh-oh!

In the meantime, God had the Israelites camping in an interesting place. They were backed up to the Red Sea. They couldn't run away on land.

When Pharaoh and his chariots and army arrived, the Israelites had no way to escape. Uh-oh again. Let's set up our own Red Sea to see if there's any advice we can give the Israelites.

Have kids help you spread your shiny blue cloth (or other blue fabric) near the middle of the room. If you brought artificial greenery, arrange it in front of your sea to create a tropical setting. Behind the blue cloth, place two tables side by side with the long sides together. Later in the story you'll tilt these tables on their sides to create walls of water.

Say: **Okay, Israelites, arrange yourselves in front of the sea. This is where God has led you. It's a nice place to camp, but I'm sorry to tell you that when the Egyptian army attacks, you have *no place to go!***

This seems like a pretty nice place to camp. God has led you here with a pillar of cloud by day and a pillar of fire by night. But guess what?

Open the door to admit the older kids who are playing the role of the Egyptian army. Invite them to stand facing the Israelites, as far away as your space will allow.

Say: **There are Egyptians on the horizon! After thinking things over, Pharaoh has changed his mind. He wants his slaves back. And so he has brought his *fierce army* to round up the Israelites and bring them back to Egypt to be slaves again. Just look at this *fierce army*. Aren't they pretty scary-looking? And you poor Israelites have no place to go!**

Ask:

• **What can you do?**

Say: **The Egyptian army got closer and more fierce looking.**

Some of the Israelites cried out to Moses, "Did you bring us out to the desert to die? You should've left us alone and let us serve the Egyptians!"

The Egyptian army got even closer. They looked even fiercer!

The Israelites thought, "There's no way we can win this battle."

Then God gave Moses a very strange message. "Don't be afraid. Just stand still and watch the Lord rescue you today. The Egyptians you see today will never be seen again. The Lord himself will fight for you. Just stay calm."

Ask:

• **What do you think of God's instructions?**

• **Tell whether you'd rather stand still and wait for God to do something or do something yourself.**

Say: **It may seem a little strange, but sometimes God's plan is for us to sit right where we are until he acts. Most of us would like to run around trying to take care of things on our own, but we need to remember this: The God who made the universe is the same ★ *God who helps us when we're in trouble.* Sometimes we can't even *imagine* what God will do! That was certainly the case in today's story.**

God had Moses stretch out his staff over the waters of the Red Sea. And then, wow! The waters began to part so there was a wall of water on both sides and dry ground in between. It looked something like this.

Have kids tip the two classroom tables so their tops form "walls of water" with a narrow opening.

Say: **Then Moses told the people, "Hurry! Go across while** the ground is dry!" So the nearly 2 million people scurried across the Red Sea on dry ground.

Have the Israelites "escape" through the space between two tables.

Say: **When the fierce Egyptian army saw what was happening, they plunged into the sea right behind the Israelites.**

Have your visiting "Egyptians" start through the walls of water, and then stop them.

Say: **Then Moses stretched his arm out over the Red Sea and the walls of water began to collapse on the pursuing Egyptians!**

To keep your Egyptian soldiers safe, have them back away from the tables you've tilted on their sides, kneel down, and cover their heads. Have your kids help you push the sides of the tables together, so there's no space between them.

Say: **The Israelites watched as the Egyptian soldiers all drowned—the waters of the Red Sea crashing down on them!**

Spread the blue cloth over the Egyptians. Then whisper a quick "thank you" and send them out of the room.

Say: **That was it! God won the battle for the Israelites— they didn't even have to lift a sword! They could hardly believe their eyes, but there it was. The water of the sea was calm once more, and there wasn't an Egyptian to be seen!**

Lead your kids in a joyous victory march around the room, complete with cheers and praises. Keep the march going until all your "Israelites" are well worn out and ready to sit down. Then gather them again in a circle.

Ask:

• **How do you feel about a plan to stay still and do nothing when a fierce army is advancing?**

• **When you first heard that the plan was for the Israelites to be still, what did you think would happen to them?**

• **If you had a choice, would you rather go back and live through that day as an Israelite or stay here? Explain.**

Say: **When God gives us instructions, "stand still" and "wait" are some of the hardest for us to hear. Most of us want to jump into action and fix things ourselves. But time after time we learn that when God tells us to be still,** ★ *God helps us when we're in trouble.*

LIFE APPLICATION

God Helps Us When We're in Trouble

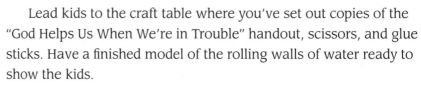

Lead kids to the craft table where you've set out copies of the "God Helps Us When We're in Trouble" handout, scissors, and glue sticks. Have a finished model of the rolling walls of water ready to show the kids.

Say: **Let's make this cool little reminder of how God made a way for the Israelites!**

Show kids how to cut out the two large pieces and then fold the waves inward on the dotted lines. Curl the waves outward by rolling them individually around pencils. Then glue the smaller wave set inside the larger wave set so the words "God helps us when we're in trouble" are showing.

Say: **Let's see—how about using these little guys to represent the Israelites marching through the Red Sea?**

Give each child a few gummy bears.

Say: **After you've marched your bears through the sea God parted, gobble them up as a treat!**

COMMITMENT

Makin' a Way for You?

Have kids bring their completed crafts and form a circle.

Say: **We know that God helped the Israelites, and ★ *God helps us when we're in trouble.***

Ask:

• **Tell about a time you asked God for help and he seemed to take a long, long time answering.**

• **How easy or difficult was it to wait?**

Jump-start these discussions by sharing faith experiences from your life. Make sure everyone feels free to talk but no one feels pressured to do so.

Say: **Thanks, everyone, for talking about how ★ *God helps us when we're in trouble.***

God Helps Us When We're in Trouble

God gave the Israelites unusual marching orders: "Stand still!" Then God parted the waters of the Red Sea and made it possible for them to escape from Pharaoh's army. Make your own model of the parting Red Sea!

Cut out the two pieces. Fold the waves in on the dotted lines; then curl them back around a pencil. Glue the smaller wave inside the larger one.

God Helps Us When We're in Trouble

Glue smaller piece between lines.

Published in *All Together Now, Volume 1* by Group Publishing, Inc., 1515 Cascade Ave., Loveland, CO 80538.

Faith Prayers

Say: **I'm going to start a prayer that goes like this. God, I believe you'll make a way...Then I'll wait quietly for someone to finish that prayer. For instance, you might say, "For Grandma to get better" or "For my dad to get a job." It's okay if there's plenty of quiet time between our prayers.**

When you feel that everyone has prayed who wants to, close the prayer.

Mumble, Grumble

LESSON AIM

To help kids understand that ★ *God wants us to be connected to him and trust him for our daily needs.*

OBJECTIVES

Kids will

✓ participate in a whining contest,

✓ experience gathering "manna" and "quail,"

✓ list the things they trust God to provide,

✓ make Manna Pots to remind them that God is always with them, and

✓ participate in a unique prayer of thanks for God's presence and provision.

BIBLE BASIS

 Exodus 15:22–16:36

How quickly we forget...

We know better than to attribute short memories of God's deliverance only to the Israelites wandering in the desert—because we know we fall into this pattern oh so quickly ourselves.

A mere three days after God's remarkable deliverance at the Red Sea, the Israelites began to feel the strain of finding sufficient food and water in the desert to support their community of nearly 2 million people. Rather than trusting in

You'll need...

☐ 2 glasses of water

☐ stick

☐ plastic tablecloth

☐ chicken-flavored crackers*

☐ table

☐ frosted corn flake cereal*

☐ sturdy, colorful yarn cut in 3- to 6-foot lengths (2 per child)

☐ duct tape

☐ cellophane tape

☐ photocopies of the "Manna Pot" handout (p. 73)

☐ scissors

☐ glue sticks

☐ markers

* Always check for allergies before serving snacks.

the provision of the God whose miracles had seen them through crisis after crisis, the Israelites once again resorted to blaming Moses for pulling them out of Egypt, where they had had plenty to eat.

Poor Moses couldn't catch a break from these ungrateful people. You'd think the drowning of Pharaoh's pursuing army at the Red Sea would buy him more than three days' credit. But no. People were thirsty. They were hungry. And apparently they weren't interested in trusting God's ability to care for them unless there were daily miracles to prove his presence and power. So, in this passage, God sets out to do just that—to offer short-sighted people daily, miraculous provision for their physical needs of food and water.

I wonder if God ever shook his head and thought, "What's it going to take to get the people to trust in me?"

The truth is that the Israelites had lived among the Egyptians for 430 years. Over the centuries, they'd become accustomed to the Egyptian's polytheistic approach to religion. Being surrounded by such a culture had to rub off. Even though the Israelites taught about and believed in Yahweh, it'd been a long time since they'd actually interacted with him as their true and living God. Now that God had them sequestered in the desert, it was time to teach them anew that he was not like the idols of the land they'd just departed. He was the great I AM, the living God whose desire was to be with his people in a daily relationship.

This dynamic relationship was already evidenced in the pillar of cloud that led them by day and the pillar of fire by night. Now he would teach his grumbling people to turn to him for their every need—even the food and water they needed to survive.

 John 6:1-35

Exodus 15:22–16:36 is another Old Testament passage that points like an arrow to Jesus, the Son of God. In the Exodus, God miraculously provides bread from heaven in the desert to sustain the lives of multitudes. In John 6, Jesus similarly miraculously provides a feast of bread in an impossible situation. In the feeding of the 5,000, Jesus sustains not only physical life but also offers to satisfy the spiritual hunger of the people: "I am the bread of life. Whoever comes to me will never be hungry again. Whoever believes in me will never be thirsty" (John 6:35). In the Lord's Prayer, when we ask for God to "give us this day our daily bread," we become connected to the people who've asked for the same thing through millennia.

All Together Now

UNDERSTANDING YOUR KIDS

There is no such thing as a child who hasn't mastered the art of whining. Most kids who rely on day-in-and-day-out care from a giving, loving parent won't have to look far beyond themselves to recognize the spirit of the whining Israelites in today's Bible story. It takes a long time to outgrow the attitude that the world is all about "me and what I need." Even some adults never get there!

Use this lesson to encourage kids to ★ *to be connected to God and trust him for their daily needs,* both large and small.

THE LESSON »

ATTENTION GRABBER

Whine-a-Thon

Greet the kids and gather them in a group.

Ask:

• **What happens at your house when you're really, really hungry and you know it's going to be a long time until dinner?**

• **How do you sound when you ask for something over and over again that your parent can't or won't give you?**

• **Why do you think we call this kind of behavior "whining"?**

Say: **I'm going to give you a few situations. I want to hear what you'd say—and *how* you'd say it—in each situation.**

• **You're very hot and thirsty, and you find out that there's no water or lemonade.**

• **You're on a trip when food and drink don't come when you expect them.**

• **You find out someone in your family already ate the last package of your very favorite after-school snack.**

• **It's lunchtime at school, you're starving, and you open your lunch to see only a half-sandwich in the bag.**

Say: **I'm curious. I wonder which of you can do the best "But I'm hungry!" whine. You might want to say something like, "M-o-m, I'm *HUN*gry," or "When are we gonna eat—I'm starving!" or "Is this all I get to eat?" or "I can't believe you ate my snack! What about me?" Choose your own words, but let me know that you want food and you're upset that there isn't any. I'll bet we have some good whiners here. Just for fun, I'll start.**

Get on your knees in front of any child and dramatically wail, **"M-o-m, I'm *HUN*gry!"**

Stand up.

Say: **I'm sure some of you can top that, so let's each have a turn.**

Allow each of the kids to perform a whine. Encourage kids to ham it up and clap for each performance.

Say: **You guys are terrific whiners when you want to be, but let me tell you, what you did today is nothing compared to what happens in our Bible story. Let's explore what happens when whiners learn ★ *God wants us to be connected to him and trust him for our daily needs.***

All Together Now

BIBLE EXPLORATION

One Nation of Whiners (Exodus 15:22–16:36)

Ask:

• **Tell about some of the great miracles God did for the people of Israel in the Bible.**

• **If God did great miracles like that for you, how long do you think you'd remember them?**

Say: **Would you believe that only** three days **after the great getaway at the Red Sea, the Israelites were already grumbling to Moses again?** Three days? Really? **Can you believe that?**

Here's what happened. After the Red Sea, Moses led the people into the wilderness. As strange as it may seem, there were no convenience stores or gas stations where they could stop for a nice, big drink of water or a slushie. In fact, there wasn't even a trickle of a stream. Not the first day... not the second day...not even the third day.

There were about 2 million people traveling with Moses. That's a lot of thirsty folks! That's a lot of little kids who need a pit stop.

Finally **they found a spring of water. As you can imagine, people rushed to take a drink.**

Take a mouthful of water from one glass; then make a terrible face and spit it right back into the glass.

Say: **One taste of the water and, thirsty as they were, they had to spit it right out. The water was nasty and undrinkable. It would've made them all sick. What a disappointment!**

Right away they started griping at Moses. "What are we supposed to do for water?" they complained.

Now I've got a couple of challenging questions for you.

Ask:

• **Earlier, Moses didn't want to lead these people. Why do you think Moses wouldn't want such a big job?**

• **What could the people have done** rather than **griping and complaining?**

Say: **God was about to use the experience of the next few days to teach the Israelites some very important lessons to remember not just for a few weeks or a few months, but** forever. **These are lessons that are still important to us today, so let's learn all we can.**

Moses knew what to do when the people complained. He turned straight to God. God showed Moses a special stick. When Moses tossed the stick into the water, the water became good to drink.

Toss your stick into the middle of the circle. Give the second cup of water to a child to taste and confirm that the water is okay to drink.

Say: **Whew! All the thirsty people got plenty to drink. But along with the water, God had Moses deliver a message. He told Moses to say to the people: "If you listen obediently to how I tell you to live in my presence and if you keep all my laws every day, I will not make you sick with the diseases that I gave to the Egyptians, for I am the Lord,** *your healer"* (Exodus 15:26, paraphrased).

Wow, that's quite a promise, isn't it?

Ask:

• What's the most important thing you heard in that promise?

Say: **In other words, God wanted to show the Israelites that he was not like the fake gods of Egypt. He was their** *real* **God. God wanted them to get in the habit of listening and obeying so he could show that he would not hurt them, but heal them. (Here's a big, important hint: You'll hear this same message from God very soon!)**

Soon Moses led the people on to a beautiful oasis with water and palm trees, where they rested for a while. Then it was off into the wilderness again, where God led them by a pillar of cloud by day and a pillar of fire by night. Before long, though, it was the same old story: They couldn't find enough food for everyone.

The people griped to Moses: "Why didn't you leave us in Egypt where there was plenty to eat? We had pots full of meat and all the bread we wanted to eat! Did you bring us out here to die?"

Oh, brother! Does that complaint sound familiar?

Ask:

• What do you think Moses should do now?

Say: **Moses turned right to God for help. God told Moses, "I'll test my people once more to see if they've learned to follow me. Then they will know that I am the Lord their God. Tonight they will eat meat and I will rain down bread from heaven."**

As Moses and Aaron explained these things to the

All Together Now

people, the bright glory of God appeared in the cloud that led them. The people were surprised and knew they should pay attention to what Moses said.

That evening, flocks of quail flew right into the camp. All the people had to do was grab them and roast them over their fires. Mmm! They might've tasted a little like roasted chicken—kind of like these chicken crackers.

"Fly" a chicken-flavored cracker toward each child.

That night, all the people went to bed in their tents. How about pretending that this table is your tent and crawling underneath it? There won't be room for everyone to lie down, so just rest your head on your knees. Please keep your eyes closed until I tell you it's morning, and give me some nice, loud snores so I know for sure that you're asleep.

Dim the lights. Spread a plastic tablecloth outside the tent area. Quietly sprinkle enough frosted corn flakes on the tablecloth so each child can have a few. Then turn on the lights and announce: It's morning!

Say: The Israelites looked outside their tents and saw dew on the ground. When the dew disappeared, there were pale, white flakes. The Israelites looked at each other and asked, "What is it?" In their language, "What is it?" sounds something like "manna." God told them just to gather a jarful of these flakes. In this case, you may gather a small handful. But be sure everyone in your tent ends up with about the same amount.

Go ahead and munch on your "manna" while I tell you about it. The Bible tells us it tasted a little like wafers made with honey. All the time the Israelites were in the wilderness, they found manna on the ground every morning.

God told them to take only what they needed to use that day. Some people disobeyed and kept some overnight. Eeeww—the next day it was full of maggots and smelled terrible! God was very unhappy that some people disobeyed.

Now on the last day of the week, just before the day of rest, God told the people they could gather two jarfuls of manna. This was because God didn't want people working to collect manna on the day of rest—he said they could get all they needed on the day before, and it wouldn't rot. And sure enough, the extra manna collected didn't rot!

Teacher Tip

If your kids won't fit under one table, let them suggest other covered areas they can use as tents.

Ask:

• Think about the things that happened to these people. What did God want them to learn?

Say: **God was changing the Israelites into people who trusted, obeyed, and relied on him. Out in the desert, far away from the fake gods of Egypt, was the perfect place to do that. Out of all the nations of the world, God had chosen the Israelites to be his special people. ★ *God wanted them to be connected to him and trust him for their daily needs.* Now it was time for the Israelites to show God that he was their special God by learning to love him, remembering that he was with them, and honoring his rules every day.**

LIFE APPLICATION
. . . .
Attached to God and Each Other

Before class cut two lengths of yarn for each child, and duct tape them securely in a single bunch to a whiteboard or a post in your teaching area. Cut the yarn in varying lengths of 3 to 6 feet.

Say: **Here's a thinking question for you. I'd like you to sit with this question quietly for a few seconds before you raise your hands. I'll keep my head down and not call on anyone until I'm sure you've had plenty of time to think this through.**

Ask:

• What in the world does all this have to do with our lives today?

Let me rephrase the question.

• How do the lessons God taught the Israelites apply to us? Or *do* they apply to us?

Let's start thinking *now*.

Put your head down and ignore any children who call out. After you're confident that kids have done some deep thinking, look up and begin to call on kids.

After kids have answered, say: **God was forming a special connection to the Israelite people, and he very much wants to have that same kind of special connection with us. Let's have some fun seeing what that connection looks like.**

Lead the kids to the bunch of yarn.

Say: **I have two tasks for you here. The first task is to finish this sentence: I know God is with me every day** because...As you finish the sentence, pick up a piece of yarn—any piece of yarn—and hold it. I'll lightly tape the yarn to one of your fingers.

Once kids give an answer, make a circle of cellophane tape to lightly attach the end of the yarn to the child's finger.

The children will end up standing in a rather tight bunch around the yarn. This is a good thing.

Say: **Good job on your first task! Here's your second. Choose a second piece of yarn with your other hand. Finish this sentence: I show my love for God each day by...**

Secure the second length of yarn with a cellophane tape loop around a finger on the second hand. Kids will end up looped and tied around each other in a tight group.

Say: **Look at yourselves!**

Ask:

• **What do you see?**

Say: **Exactly! Do you know that you've just demonstrated what God wanted from the Israelites? First, you've come together as a people of God. Second, you've told God that you're aware that he's with you every day and that your love for him is going to make a difference in the way you think and act. How cool is that? You've just learned in a few minutes what it took the Israelites many, many long years to begin to understand: that ★** *God wants us to be connected to him and trust him for our daily needs.* **Good job!**

Carefully remove the duct tape from the post or the whiteboard. Ask children to keep the yarn attached to their fingers for a little while longer.

COMMITMENT

. . . .

Manna Pot

Lead kids to the craft table where you've set out scissors, glue sticks, and copies of the "Manna Pot" handout. Have a finished sample of the Manna Pot available and pass it around. Have older kids sit by younger kids to assist with assembly of the Manna Pot.

Say: **Today we're going to make Manna Pots that'll help us remember what God taught the Israelites in the desert: that ★** *God wants us to be connected to him and trust him for our daily needs.*

The finished project may look complicated, but it's

Teacher Tip

There's a fair amount of cutting with this project. You might ask an older child or an assistant to cut the pieces apart ahead of time. Then store the pieces in individual resealable bags.

actually very easy to assemble. Let's work on each step together.

- ✓ Cut out the Manna Pot pieces, the base, and the Manna Pot tag.
- ✓ Fold the base in half the long way in order to cut a slit on the line marked at the center. Then unfold and flatten the base.
- ✓ Fold in the long tabs on the two Manna Pot pieces. Rub glue on the tabs, and stick the halves together to form a pocket.
- ✓ Stick the narrow tabs of the Manna Pot through the slit in the base. Fold the tabs back, and glue them to the back of the base.
- ✓ Write your name on the Manna Pot tag. Fold the tag in half; then unfold and glue it to the back of the base, so it covers the base tabs of the Manna Pot.

When everyone has assembled Manna Pots, say: **Now tuck your pieces of yarn from our previous activity inside your little Manna Pots. They'll remind you that ★ God wants you to be connected to him and trust him for your daily needs.**

CLOSING

Examen

Say: **Checking in with God at the end of the day is an ancient practice in Christianity called** *examen.* **I'll show you how you can use these little Manna Pots you've made to join Christians over the centuries in practicing the ancient discipline of** *examen.*

You probably recognize the two phrases printed next to the Manna Pot as similar to the ones we completed when we held the pieces of yarn. So you've already practiced how simple this is!

Place your little Manna Pot by your bedside. Before you say your prayers at night, finish the phrases written on your Manna Pot. You could do this with your mom or dad or all by yourself. It would even be cool for your whole family to do it together! It's just a quick way to check on how you're ★ connected to God and depend on him to take care of your daily needs!

Tell me how you'll use this to explain to your families that God takes care of us. Allow time for kids' responses; then say: **Good job! I'll see you next time!**

All Together Now

Manna Pot

Manna Pot pieces

1. Cut out the Manna Pot pieces, the base, and the tag.
2. Fold the base in half lengthwise in order to cut the slit on the line marked at the center. Then unfold and flatten the base.
3. Fold in the long tabs on the two Manna Pot pieces. Rub glue stick on the tabs, and stick the two halves together to form a pocket.
4. Stick the narrow tabs of the Manna Pot through the slit in the base. Fold the tabs back, and glue them to the back of the base.
5. Write your name on the Manna Pot tag. Fold the tag in half; then unfold and glue it to the back of the base, so it covers the base tabs of the Manna Pot.

Manna Pot tag

_____'s

MANNA POT

Manna Pot base

I showed my love for God today when...

I knew that God was with me today when...

Published in *All Together Now, Volume 1* by Group Publishing, Inc., 1515 Cascade Ave., Loveland, CO 80538.

73

Carried on Wings of Love

You'll need...

- ☐ bag of colorful plastic gems, including at least 1 purple jewel per child
- ☐ resealable snack bags
- ☐ noisemaker
- ☐ small jewelry box or basket
- ☐ shawl
- ☐ "Caravanserai," from Loreena McKennitt's album *An Ancient Muse*, or "Egypt Soundtrack" from Group's Egypt VBS (available at group.com), or other thoughtful instrumental music
- ☐ 3 or more battery-powered candles
- ☐ visiting storyteller wearing Bible-times costume *(optional)*
- ☐ CD player
- ☐ photocopies of the "Really Cool Letter From God" handout (p. 80)
- ☐ scissors
- ☐ pens
- ☐ straws or Pixy Stix candies*
- ☐ bottle of craft glue
- ☐ paper cutter *(optional)*

* Always check for allergies before serving snacks.

LESSON AIM

To help kids recognize that throughout their lives, ★ *God has lovingly brought us to him.*

OBJECTIVES

Kids will

- ✓ participate in a treasure hunt,
- ✓ listen to a quiet telling of the Bible story,
- ✓ create a simple journal of ways God has lovingly brought them to him, and
- ✓ receive a jewel as a reminder of how precious they are to God.

BIBLE BASIS

 Exodus 19

This Scripture is one that's seldom emphasized. In terms of spiritual formation for children, it's one of the true gems in the Word of God. Although God is the maker of the moon and stars, and indeed the whole universe, he chose a special people at a special time and brought them to him ever so gently, as an eagle would carry her young.

Those words apply to us who have become part of God's covenant with Israel by faith. Those words apply to each child. And to you as well, beloved of God, who give of yourself so freely to share God's grace with his little ones.

All Together Now

These words in Exodus 19 are the prologue to the much more famous Ten Commandments, which follow in Exodus 20. The fact that God provides this beautiful love song to Israel (and to us) before beginning with the stern-sounding "thou shalt nots" makes all the difference!

Look up an image of Mount Horeb, one of the possible locations of Mount Sinai, in the southern area of the Sinai peninsula. You'll see that the Israelites had the most barren and stark of landscapes in which to await God's Word to them. Soon the mountain itself would begin to belch fire and shake, and anyone who even approached the mountain's perimeter would die. How they needed these gentle words from God, assuring them that of all people in the world, he'd specifically chosen them to be holy and special!

📖 **Galatians 3:6–9, 26–29**

The Jews remained God's special people—set apart in their laws, the way they dressed, ate, spoke, and worshipped—until Jesus came and opened the way to God for all who'd believe in him. Jesus declared a "new covenant" in his blood during the Last Supper. As hard as it was for the Jews to accept, the house of Abraham was suddenly open not to those born of a certain family or who followed a certain group of customs, but to anyone who accepted *by faith* the sacrifice of Jesus' blood spilled on the cross as the sacrifice for sins that ended all sacrifices.

When the curtain in the sanctuary of the Temple ripped apart at the crucifixion of our Savior (see Matthew 27:51), the way to God became open to all. And all who responded became the beloved of God, the receivers of the promises given to God's people long ago.

UNDERSTANDING YOUR KIDS

It's vital for kids to know how special they are in God's eyes. There are so many ways for kids to feel unlovely—glasses, freckles, hair that sticks out, hair that doesn't stick out, lack of coordination, shyness, big feet, tiny feet, and on goes the list. Are you identifying with any of these from your childhood days or for any of the kids in your ministry? Big *ouch* right in the heart, yes?

Today's lesson will be an especially great opportunity for you to open kids' eyes to ways each of them is a gem in God's eyes, a precious possession, one he's wooed throughout their lifetimes and carried to his side.

ATTENTION GRABBER

My Greatest Treasure

Before class, scatter a large bag of plastic craft gems around the room in less-than-obvious places.

Greet the kids and say: **Who's up for a treasure hunt today?**
Give each of the kids a resealable bag.

Say: **Here's how our treasure hunt works. When you find a pile of treasure, don't take it all for yourself. We want everybody to find some treasure. Once you've found treasure in one place, don't go looking in other places. You don't need a great big pile—a nice little stash in your bag will do just fine.**

If you're having trouble finding treasure, don't get frustrated. Just look for kids who've already found some. I'm sure those kids will be willing to show you their stash and share it with you. Any questions?

Okay, when I blow my noisemaker (demonstrate your noisemaker)**, please come back to the circle with the treasure you've collected. Ready, set...go!**

When it looks like everyone has a fair amount of treasure in his or her bag, blow your noisemaker to bring kids back to your circle. Have kids show off their glittering treasure.

Say: **Wow! Congratulations on finding all that loot!**
Bring out your treasure box—a small jewelry box or basket.

Say: **What I didn't tell you before is that the *purple jewels* are much more highly valued than jewels of any other color. In fact, all the rest of the jewels in the room don't equal the value of a single purple jewel. Imagine that! So quickly sort through your jewels and find all the purple ones. Bring them to me and put them into my treasure box for safekeeping.**

"Ooh" and "ahh" over the beauty of the purple jewels as kids bring them to you. Then show the treasure box to the kids and let them admire the purple jewels. Remark on their great beauty and value, and praise the kids for their treasure-hunting abilities.

Say: **Thank you for bringing me your special purple jewels. Today we will learn how ★ *God has lovingly brought us to him!***

Separate the kids from the rest of their jewels at this point so they won't be a distraction. You may want to collect the jewels for future projects, or allow kids to keep a few for fun. Kids will each receive one very special purple jewel before going home.

All Together Now

BIBLE EXPLORATION

On Eagles' Wings (Exodus 19)

Say: **Please get ready for today's Bible story by spreading out a bit and lying on the floor facing the center of our story circle. Make yourself nice and comfy. I'm going to dim the lights and turn on a few candles. As I do, please quiet yourselves and prepare to hear God's Word—a message that came first to the Israelites and now to you. Let's make this a holy time, set apart for God.**

Play the first two minutes of the song "Caravanserai" from Loreena McKennitt's album *An Ancient Muse* as kids settle. (Lyrics begin at about 2:19, so if you want more than two minutes of music, restart it from the beginning.) Another great song you can use is the "Egypt Soundtrack" from Group's Egypt VBS, available at group.com. Darken your room as much as possible. Turn on a battery-powered candle in the middle of your circle. Turn on two other candles and place them where they'll cast a gentle glow over the room.

When the scene is set, say: **I'm going to pray something like a Jewish person would pray—that God will be with us for this very special Bible story. My prayer will be silent. I invite you to join me in silent prayer.**

Pull a shawl over your head, cover your face with your hands, and rock forward and backward gently in the manner of Jewish prayer at the Eastern Wall as you ask God to be present with you and your children as you teach. When you've finished, pull off your head covering and address the children quietly. Walk around the edge of the circle and create an air of mystery as you tell the Bible story.

Say: **Two months had passed since that fateful night when the children of Israel walked away from their lives of slavery in Egypt and began to follow God in the wilderness. God led them with a pillar of cloud by day and a pillar of fire by night, so wherever they went the Israelites knew that God was right there watching over them.**

Each morning God sent a dusting of manna over the camp. The people could gather all they needed to eat. Every night God sent plump quail they could roast over open camp fires.

Ask kids to reflect in silence about how God led the Israelites out of Egypt.

Say: **By this time the Israelites realized that God was different from the idols and fake gods of Egypt. God was real.**

> ## Teacher Tip
> Though this is a simple story, you may wish to invite a skilled storyteller from your congregation to visit in a Bible-times costume and tell it.

God was there with them, and God showed his care for them day after day without fail.

Finally the Israelites' travels brought them through the wilderness of Sinai to the foot of Mount Horeb, the very mountain where Moses had seen the burning bush and received God's call to lead the slaves out of Egypt so long ago. This was no ordinary mountain. Oh, no. This was a holy mountain where God's presence dwelled. There were no green pastures for camping—just a rocky wilderness that led right up to the steep, stony cliffs of the mountain itself. No one dared go near the mountain for sometimes it would tremble and smoke with the very presence of God. God warned Moses that anyone who touched the base of the mountain would surely die.

Ask kids to imagine the steepest, hottest, and most barren and rocky mountain they can think of.

Say: **Only Moses could go up the mountain to listen to God. And when he did, God gave him a very surprising message for the people. Because we are now God's people through faith in Jesus, the message is for us, too. You might think it would be a strong, scary message. In fact, it's just the opposite. It's like a love note from a caring, wonderful father. Please close your eyes while I read God's message to you.**

> Give these instructions to the family of Jacob; announce it to the descendants of Israel: "You have seen what I did to the Egyptians. You know how I carried you on eagles' wings and brought you to myself. Now if you will obey me and keep my covenant, you will be my own special treasure from among all the peoples on earth; for all the earth belongs to me. And you will be my kingdom of priests, my holy nation." This is the message you must give to the people of Israel. (Exodus 19:3-6)

...and to my children: [name all the children present].

Invite kids to sit up.

Say: **I'm going to read the message once more. Listen carefully and see what stands out to you.** Read Exodus 19:3-6 again.

Ask:

• **What stands out to you in that message?**

• **Why do you think an awesome, powerful God sent such a beautiful, loving message to his people and to us?**

All Together Now

• **If you were there in the desert and saw Moses go up the mountain to listen to God and then heard him come down with this message, what would you think?**

Say: **Just as he did with the Israelites, ★** *God has lovingly brought each of us to him.*

LIFE APPLICATION
....
Really Cool Letter From God

Say: **You're going to have a chance to respond to God's message, right here, right now. Unlike some of our activities, this isn't going to be fun and rowdy. We're going to keep the same special, quiet tone that we did during our Bible story.**

First we're going to make an easy, very cool journal.

Restore some of the lights in the room, but not all. Direct kids to the craft table where you've set out copies of the "Really Cool Letter From God" handout, scissors, straws or Pixy Stix candies, and pens.

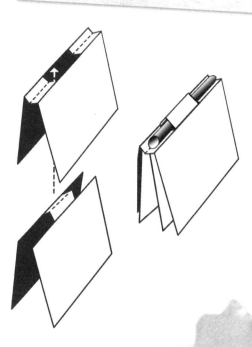

- ✓ Have kids write their names on the three blank lines on the handout.

- ✓ Show kids how to fold the halves of the journal at the center and cut away the darkened areas.

- ✓ Place the title page on the outside. Slip the center pages inside with the Exodus 19 passage as page 2.

- ✓ Weave a straw or Pixy Stix candy through the fold that's sticking up in the middle to form a spine.

- ✓ Smooth the other pages so the journal lies flat.

- ✓ If you have children use Pixy Stix candies, let them enjoy a couple of extras for treats.

Say: **This is actually a very ancient way of putting books together. Now that your journals are together, please read through them and answer the questions very thoughtfully. When everyone has finished, I'll have something special for you to add to your journal.**

As kids work, mingle among them, encouraging them to tell you about their answers.

Teacher Tip

To save time, you may want to cut apart the two pieces of this handout with a paper cutter ahead of time.

Teacher Tip

Have an assistant or an older child sit with younger children and help with reading and writing answers to the journal questions.

Really Cool Letter From God

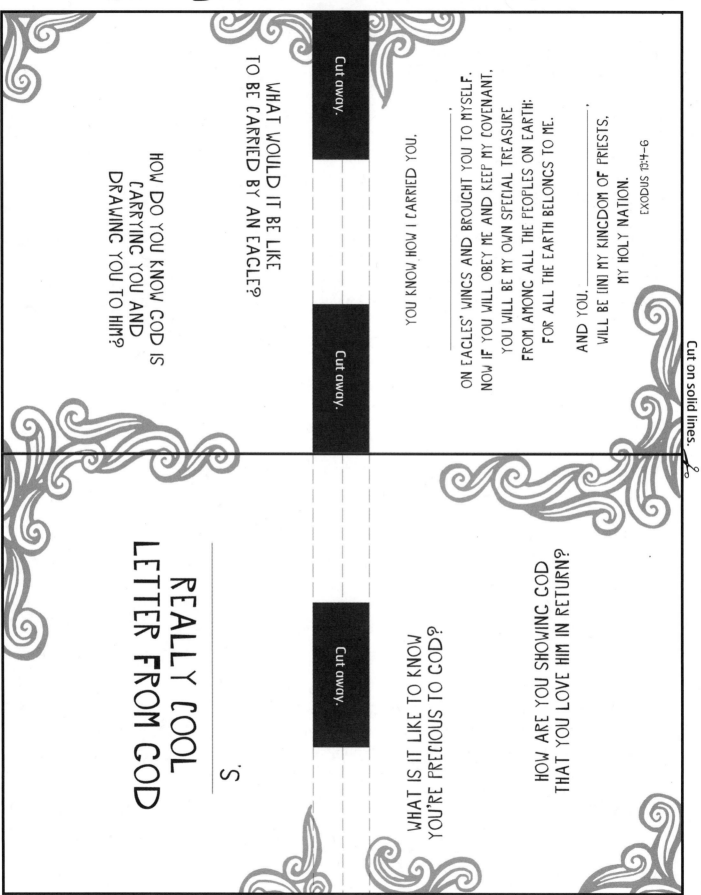

Cut away.

WHAT WOULD IT BE LIKE
TO BE CARRIED BY AN EAGLE?

YOU KNOW HOW I CARRIED YOU,

ON EAGLES' WINGS AND BROUGHT YOU TO MYSELF.
NOW IF YOU WILL OBEY ME AND KEEP MY COVENANT,
YOU WILL BE MY OWN SPECIAL TREASURE
FROM AMONG ALL THE PEOPLES ON EARTH;
FOR ALL THE EARTH BELONGS TO ME.

AND YOU, _____
WILL BE [IN] MY KINGDOM OF PRIESTS,
MY HOLY NATION.

EXODUS 19:4-6

Cut away.

Cut on solid lines.

HOW DO YOU KNOW GOD IS
CARRYING YOU AND
DRAWING YOU TO HIM?

REALLY COOL
LETTER FROM GOD

_____'S

Cut away.

WHAT IS IT LIKE TO KNOW
YOU'RE PRECIOUS TO GOD?

HOW ARE YOU SHOWING GOD
THAT YOU LOVE HIM IN RETURN?

Published in *All Together Now, Volume 1* by Group Publishing, Inc., 1515 Cascade Ave., Loveland, CO 80538.

COMMITMENT

Precious Jewels

Say: **Please let me know when you've completed your journal by placing it in front of you and putting your hands in your lap.**

When a child completes a journal, take your treasure box of purple jewels and a bottle of craft glue to that child's place. Glue a purple jewel near the child's name on the cover and say: [Child's name], **you are precious to God. He will carry you tenderly on eagles' wings and bring you to him.**

Repeat the affirmation and jewel placement with each child. Then invite kids to open their journals to the question about being carried by an eagle, and ask:

• **What do you think it would be like to be carried on an eagle's wings?**

• **In what ways do you know that God is always carrying you, bringing you to him?**

• **What's it like to be precious to God?**

• **What are some ways you can remember that you're precious to God?**

Say: **Here's an idea I'd like you to do: Someday when you're feeling really awful, when everything has gone wrong, when it just feels like the world is against you, pick up this journal and read through it. Touch the purple jewel and remember that you're precious to God. Traditionally, purple is the color of royalty, the highest of all colors. And you are most definitely precious to God. Read through his promise to you, and remember that ★ God has lovingly brought us to him.**

CLOSING

Blessing

Gather kids in a circle with their completed journals.

Say: **Hold your journals in your open hands as I close with prayer.**

Dear God, you who love us more than we can imagine, thank you for loving us before we were even born. Thank you for carrying us on eagles' wings and continuing to draw us to you every day of our lives. We pray in Jesus' name, amen.

The Covenant

You'll need...

- ☐ whiteboard or newsprint
- ☐ markers
- ☐ large plastic tarp
- ☐ Sticky Tack removable adhesive (available at office supply stores) or masking tape
- ☐ baking sheets, large pots, wooden spoons
- ☐ 2 pieces of dark gray drawing paper or poster board
- ☐ pencils
- ☐ scissors
- ☐ paper towel tube or toy horn
- ☐ photocopies of the "Ten Commandments Rally" handout (p. 90)
- ☐ paper cutter
- ☐ 4 photocopies of the "Road Rally Banner" (p. 89)
- ☐ 3 quart-size resealable bags
- ☐ 40-inch length of twine for each child
- ☐ cellophane tape

LESSON AIM

To help kids see that ★ *God gave us laws to guide and protect us.*

OBJECTIVES

Kids will

- ✓ imagine life without some basic rules,
- ✓ go on a road rally to discover the Ten Commandments,
- ✓ assemble a rally banner to remember the laws of God's covenant, and
- ✓ learn that Jesus said the greatest commandment is to love God and to love our neighbors as ourselves.

BIBLE BASIS

 **Exodus 19:10—20:21**

In the first part of Exodus 19, we see God's tender love. In the second part of the chapter and in Exodus 20, we see God's mighty holiness. We see in God's acts and words that the extraordinary love he lavished on the people of Israel demanded their exclusive faithfulness.

In the Ten Commandments, God lays out the terms of the covenant relationship he's been forming with the people since first making himself known to them as their rescuer in the land of Egypt. On the Israelites' behalf, God defeated the most

All Together Now

powerful ruler on earth. For their survival God provided guidance in the wilderness as well as daily bread and meat.

God knew that the Promised Land (then in the possession of the Canaanites and others) would be full of false gods worshipped as idols. To prepare the people to deal with that idolatry, God kept them in the wilderness, before his holy mountain, to make these sons and daughters of Abraham his own, so that their faith would be only in him, their loyalty only to him.

Exodus 20:1-17 sets out the Ten Commandments in two basic groups. The first group deals with how God expects humans to relate to him: to have no other gods, to make no idols or graven images, to refrain from misusing the name of the Lord, and to observe the Sabbath. The second group of commandments focuses on a code of conduct between humans: honor parents, do not murder, do not commit adultery, do not steal, be honest, do not covet others' possessions. This essential code of conduct has served as the basis for human legal codes for millennia.

📖 Matthew 22:35-40

In this passage, the Sadducees and Pharisees, who weren't the best of friends, had found a common "enemy" in Jesus and converged on him to trip him up in his teaching. Can you see them huddling together, doing their best to come up with questions to ensnare Jesus? This peasant from Galilee was stealing their thunder and they just had to find a way to put him in his place. But on this and many other occasions, Jesus not only turned the tables on them, but he also taught a landmark truth in the process. "Teacher," they asked, "which is the most important commandment in the law of Moses?" The question was intended to force Jesus to choose one of the commandments, and then they'd accuse him of disrespecting all of the other commandments.

Instead, Jesus flipped the question and gave an irrefutable answer: " 'You must love the Lord your God with all your heart, all your soul, and all your mind.' This is the first and greatest commandment. A second is equally important: 'Love your neighbor as yourself.' " Now those are words to live by.

UNDERSTANDING YOUR KIDS

It may be a few years before your kids are ready to rejoice over the existence of rules. As adults we've learned to embrace them for safety and order—right up until red and blue law enforcement lights flash in our rearview mirrors for some of us.

Use this lesson to help your kids see that God gave the Ten Commandments for the safety and protection of his people and to establish his exclusive relationship with them among the cultures who worshipped numerous gods. Also help them understand that Jesus' summary of the commandments (loving God and loving others) is the perfect guideline for their lives.

All Together Now

ATTENTION GRABBER

THE LESSON

Away With the Rules!

Greet kids and say: **Let's put together a list of rules you have at home and at school.** Jot down on a whiteboard the rules kids mention, keeping separate columns for home and school. Let each child contribute at least one rule for each column. Kids may be surprised to hear some of the same rules at each other's homes.

Once you have a fairly lengthy set of rules, say: **Hmm...I think you're going to like this next part.**

Ask:

• **Suppose that, just for the sake of imagination, you could get rid of a rule you really didn't like. What rule would you get rid of first—and why?**

Some kids may be very excited about getting rid of rules. More compliant kids may not want to get rid of any at all. After kids name a rule they want to get rid of, say: **Okay, let's get rid of this rule.** Cross a line through the unwanted rule so it's still legible. Keep going until kids have banished all the rules they don't like.

Say: **This is a very different set of rules from the one we started with.**

Ask:

• **If we lived for a month or two without the rules we got rid of, what do you think would change?**

Say: **I have rules for myself, too.** List your rules on the board where kids can read them. Here are starter ideas for what you might include, but it's best to come up with ideas of your own. (1) Don't pass on gossip about people. (2) Start supper before sitting down to read a favorite book. (3) Don't explode at my kids and call them names even if I'm really angry. (4) Get along with someone who works with me even though I don't always like his attitude. (5) Don't leave a nasty note for an annoying neighbor. (6) Don't act like I don't notice if a sales clerk gives me too much change. (7) Don't honk at a confused driver in front of me.

Let's see: I'm going to knock a few rules off my list.

Cross off several rules from the list and explain why they're not your favorite rules.

Ask:

• **If I went for a month or two without these rules, what kinds of things do you think might happen?**

• **Why do you think we have rules?**

• **What do you like about rules?**

Volume 1—FALL ★ Lesson 8   85

Say: **Rules actually make our lives better. They give us order and keep us safe. That's a good thing to think about as we look at ★ _the rules God gave us to guide and protect us._**

BIBLE EXPLORATION

. . . .

Ten Commandments Rally (Exodus 20:1-21)

Before class, make enough copies of the "Ten Commandments Rally" handout for each child to have one. Using a paper cutter, cut the command banners apart on the dotted lines, so that 1 and 2 are together, 3 and 4 are together, and so on. The kids will complete the cutting later. Place the banners for commandments 1 through 4 in one resealable bag, 5 through 8 in another, and 9 and 10 in another. Set the bags aside, keeping the commandments in order.

Plan where you will hide the three bags of commandments for your road rally. Write the directions to the first bag on the back of a rally banner. For instance, you might write, "Turn left down the hall, right into the fellowship room, and look in the first bottom cabinet." On the first bag of commandments, attach a rally banner with directions to the second bag of commandments. For instance, you might write, "Leave the fellowship room by the double doors, go right to the stairway, go up the stairs, turn left, and look behind a large plant." On the third bag of commandments, attach a rally banner with directions to return to the classroom.

Say: **The Israelites were camping in front of Mount Sinai. Everybody say that with me: Mount Sinai. There's one thing we know about Mount Sinai—when God was present, it wasn't a quiet mountain. Let's see what that might've been like.**

Stack four or five chairs together to form a mountain. Start with a circle of chairs on the bottom to ensure the structure is sturdy. Then hand kids a large plastic tarp.

Say: **Let's use this tarp to cover the front part of our mountain to make it look more real.**

Hand out small pieces of Sticky Tack removable adhesive or masking tape. Have kids use the adhesive or tape to secure the tarp to the floor and chairs.

Say: **That looks great! Now we need a couple of artists to quickly draw and cut out some dark, smoky clouds.**

Give artists pencils, poster board, and scissors to work on clouds.

Say: **The rest of you will be special effects people. Help me move these baking sheets, large pots, and wooden spoons behind the mountain. Today's Bible passage will tell about Mount Sinai shaking with thunder and lightning.**

Ask:

• **How can you use these props as special effects to make thunder and lightning?**

Say: **Make room for the dark, thunderous clouds that are about to join us, too.**

Make sure each child has a prop to use behind Mount Sinai.

Say: **You're looking good! Now listen carefully as I tell the story straight from the Bible. Use your props when it's appropriate, and then stop. Ready?**

"Then the Lord told Moses, 'Go down and prepare the people for my arrival. Consecrate them today and tomorrow, and have them wash their clothing. Be sure they are ready on the third day, for on that day the Lord will come down on Mount Sinai as all the people watch. Mark off a boundary all around the mountain.' "

Mark off an imaginary boundary around your mountain. Have kids circle the mountain outside of the boundary.

Say: **"Warn the people, 'Be careful! Do not go up on the mountain or even touch its boundaries. Anyone who touches the mountain will certainly be put to death. No hand may touch the person or animal that crosses the boundary; instead, stone them or shoot them with arrows. They must be put to death.' However, when the ram's horn sounds a long blast, then the people may go up on the mountain."**

Have kids repeat, "God is serious about this!"

Say: **"On the morning of the third day, thunder roared and lightning flashed, and a dense cloud came down on the mountain. There was a long, loud blast from a ram's horn, and all the people trembled."**

Have kids make storm noises. Blow the horn or paper towel roll. Have kids shake with fear.

Say: **"Moses led them out from the camp to meet with God, and they stood at the foot of the mountain. All of Mount Sinai was covered with smoke because the Lord had descended on it in the form of fire. The smoke billowed into the sky like smoke from a brick kiln, and the whole mountain shook violently."**

Have kids make storm noises and shake the mountain.

Say: **"As the blast of the ram's horn grew louder and louder, Moses spoke, and God thundered his reply. The Lord came down on the top of Mount Sinai and called Moses to the top of the mountain. So Moses climbed the mountain."**

Have kids keep shaking the mountain and making storm noises. Blow the horn again.

Say: **"Then God gave the people all these instructions: 'I am the Lord your God, who rescued you from the land of Egypt, the place of your slavery. You must not have any other god but me. You must not make for yourself an idol of any kind or an image of anything in the heavens or on the earth or in the sea. You must not bow down to them or worship them, for I, the Lord your God, am a jealous God who will not tolerate your affection for any other gods…You must not misuse the name of the Lord your God…Remember to observe the Sabbath day by keeping it holy…For in six days the Lord made the heavens, the earth, the sea, and everything in them; but on the seventh day he rested…Honor your father and mother…You must not murder…You must not commit adultery. You must not steal. You must not testify falsely against your neighbor. You must not covet your neighbor's house…or anything else that belongs to your neighbor.' When the people heard the thunder and the loud blast of the ram's horn, and when they saw the flashes of lightning and the smoke billowing from the mountain, they stood at a distance, trembling with fear. And they said to Moses, 'You speak to us, and we will listen. But don't let God speak directly to us, or we will die!' "**

Have kids repeat: "You speak to us, and we will listen. But don't let God speak directly to us, or we will die!"

When you've finished reading, ask kids to leave their props behind the mountain and join you in a circle.

Ask:

• **What happened when God spoke?**

• **What would you think if you heard God speak out loud right now?**

Say: **During all that noise, we passed quickly over a very important section of the Bible. The Ten Commandments form the very foundation of our society. ★** *God gave us laws to guide and protect us.* **These laws help us live together safely, loving God and each other the way God planned. I have a fun way for us to find out more about the Ten Commandments—let's do a Road Rally!**

All Together Now

Ten Commandments Rally

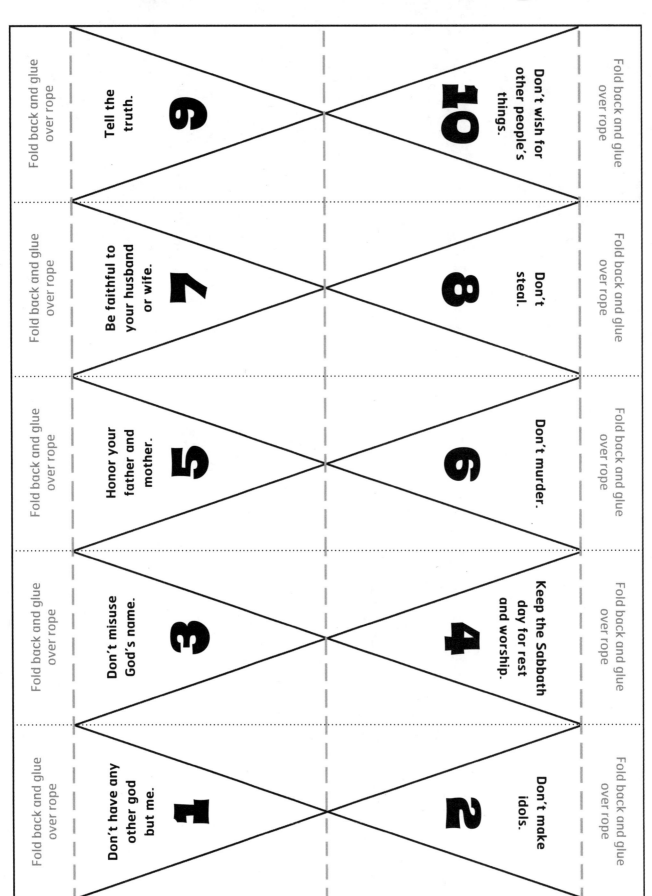

Fold back and glue over rope

Tell the truth.

9

Don't wish for other people's things.

10

Fold back and glue over rope

Fold back and glue over rope

Be faithful to your husband or wife.

7

Don't steal.

8

Fold back and glue over rope

Fold back and glue over rope

Honor your father and mother.

5

Don't murder.

6

Fold back and glue over rope

Fold back and glue over rope

Don't misuse God's name.

3

Keep the Sabbath day for rest and worship.

4

Fold back and glue over rope

Fold back and glue over rope

Don't have any other god but me.

1

Don't make idols.

2

Fold back and glue over rope

Pull out the banner with the directions to the first bag of commandment banners.

Say: **On the back of this banner are the directions to our first rally point. As we travel there, remember that there are other classes meeting. So even though we're having tons of fun, we'll need to be quiet and not disturb anyone else.**

Have kids line up at the door and choose a child to read the directions to the first rally point. The reader will also be the Captain of this part of the rally. Say: **The Captain will lead us. No running ahead of the Captain.**

When you reach the first rally point, choose another child to distribute the first four commandments. Gather kids in a group on the floor. Have a few volunteers read the commandments out loud.

After you've read through them, say: **There's a common key that ties these four commandments together. I wonder if you can discover what it is. This is a thinking question, so don't answer right away. You have one minute to think it over.**

When time is up, ask:
- **Why do you think God gave us rules that relate to him?**
- **Why is it important to follow these rules?**

Choose a second Captain to read the directions on the back of the rally banner and lead kids to the second rally point. Here, ask another volunteer to distribute commandments 5 through 8. Again, have kids read them aloud.

Ask:
- **Here comes the same thinking question: One thing ties these commandments together. Can you discover what it is?**

Give kids one minute to think. Then ask:
- **Why do you think God gave us rules about how to get along with other people?**
- **Why do you think it's important to follow these rules?**

Choose a third Captain to read the directions on the back of the rally banner and lead kids to the third rally point. Ask for a volunteer to distribute commandments 9 and 10, and other kids to volunteer to read them aloud.

Say: **These two commandments are also about getting along with people.**

Choose another Captain to read the instructions that'll guide you back to your room.

Ask:

• **Why do you think God gave us so many rules that have to do with getting along with other people?**

Say: **Some people through history have felt that the Ten Commandments were God's way of ruining their fun or bossing their life. But that's not what God intended. Instead** ★ *God gave us laws to guide and protect us.*

LIFE APPLICATION

Commandment Banners

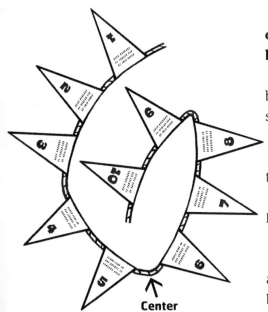

Center

Guide kids and their commandment banners to a craft table where you've set out scissors, 40-inch lengths of twine, and cellophane tape.

Say: **Fold your commandment banners in half carefully on the broken light gray line so you can cut out two of the banners at the same time. Cut on all the solid black lines.**

Demonstrate each step for the kids. Show them how to fold back the flap at the top of each banner and trim the edges that show.

Next, space your 10 banners out evenly in front of you.

Put commandments 5 and 6 in the middle; then work your way to the ends.

When you have them evenly spaced, pick up a piece of twine. Fold the twine in half and pinch it to find the middle.

Place the pinch in the twine between commandments 5 and 6.

Loop the tabs of the commandment banners over the twine, and tape them in place. Continue until all of your commandment banners are taped evenly across the twine.

As kids work, ask questions such as:

• **How do the Ten Commandments make you feel safe?**

• **Tell which commandment you're really glad God included in the Ten Commandments.**

• **How would our lives be different without the Ten Commandments?**

As kids finish, encourage them to tell you where they'll display their Ten Commandments banners in their homes.

All Together Now

COMMITMENT

....

The Heart of the Matter

Have kids spread their completed banners in front of them.
Ask:

• **Which of these commandments do you think is most important?**

Say: **That was a question someone asked Jesus to try to trick him.**

There were important teachers in Jerusalem who were jealous of Jesus. People were always amazed by the way Jesus taught. These teachers thought *they* should be the important ones—not Jesus. So they tried to trip up Jesus with tricky questions. They thought if they could catch Jesus in a wrong answer, Jesus would be embarrassed and people would stop listening to him.

So one of these teachers asked Jesus a question similar to the one I just asked you. "Which is the first and greatest commandment?" he asked.

Jesus gave a surprisingly simple and wonderful answer:

"You must love the Lord your God with all your heart, all your soul, and all your mind." This is the first and greatest commandment. A second is equally important: "Love your neighbor as yourself." (Matthew 22:37-39)

Let's think about what Jesus said for a minute.
Ask:

• **How did Jesus sum up the Ten Commandments in his answer above?**

• **Why do you think loving God with all your heart, soul, and mind is the most important commandment?**

• **Why do you think loving your neighbor as yourself is equally important?**

Say: **Isn't that something? Jesus summed up all of the commandments in two simple statements about love! Take a moment to arrange your banners into a heart shape.**

Ask:

• **Why do you think it's so important for us to love God and love each other?**

The Way of Love

Say: **Place a hand inside the heart shape you've created. Let's take turns telling one way you'll love God and one way you'll love your neighbors this week.**

After each child speaks, have kids help each other tie their banners around their necks like necklaces.

Say: ★ *God gave us laws to guide and protect us.* **Use your banner necklaces at home as conversation starters with your families. Teach them what you've learned about the Ten Commandments today.**

The God We Can't See

LESSON AIM

To help kids learn that ★ *God wants us to worship him even though we can't see him.*

OBJECTIVES

Kids will

✓ guess about things they can't see,

✓ hear the Bible story from an actor playing Aaron,

✓ make a craft encouraging them to worship God with their families, and

✓ commit to worshipping God with their families.

BIBLE BASIS

 **Exodus 32**

Habits of 430 years are hard to break.

During their time of slavery in Egypt, the Israelites knew of Yahweh, the God of their fathers, the God of Abraham, but they were accustomed to seeing idol worship throughout the vast land where they served. One such idol, Hapi the bull, was supposed to be the god of the Nile River.

The chronology of Exodus can be a bit confusing in this section. In Exodus 20 and following, God gave Moses the Ten Commandments and other laws orally. Moses took all God's instructions and wrote them in the Book of the Covenant (Exodus 24:4-7). When he read the law to the people, they

You'll need...

☐ blindfolds

☐ quick-baking frozen pizza*

☐ pizza pan

☐ pizza cutter

☐ paper towels

☐ an actor to play Aaron and a Bible-times costume

☐ photocopy of "Aaron's Lament" script (pp. 101-103)

☐ photocopies of "Family Worship Challenge" handout (p. 105)

☐ pens

☐ marshmallows*

☐ pretzel rods* (broken in half)

☐ scissors

☐ string

☐ resealable sandwich bags

☐ hole punch

Always check for allergies before serving snacks.

solemnly agreed to follow everything God had told them. Then God called Moses back up the mountain. Here, God promised he would write all these laws on tablets of stone. Moses and Joshua went up the mountain, leaving Aaron and Hur in charge of the people.

As Moses' stay on the mountain with God grew longer and longer, the Israelites began to worry. They longed for the familiarity and comfort of an idol they could worship—this whole idea of a God who appeared, disappeared, and then reappeared still felt quite foreign to them. As Moses' absence grew to more than a month, their anxiety increased. Finally they demanded of Aaron an idol to worship.

Aaron, too, was new at his job. He wasn't the leader Moses was—only Moses' mouthpiece. Worried about losing control of the people, Aaron caved in to their wishes and created an idol of a golden calf. Seeing that the people were pleased, he called for a festival the next day. The people were overjoyed. They offered sacrifices, held a feast, and then partied hard. God saw the disobedient activity of his rebellious people and sent Moses and Joshua down Mount Sinai to deal with them.

Moses' anger upon seeing the people dancing around an idol resulted in the famous breaking of the God-written tablets of stone on the mountainside. But his ensuing intervention on the Israelites' behalf convinced God not to destroy them completely.

📖 John 4:21-24

Jesus' encounter with the woman at the well is eye-opening on many levels, with his teaching about how to worship God not being the least of them. The Samaritans and Jews had an ongoing disagreement about the appropriate place to worship God—the Temple Mount in Jerusalem or Mount Gerizim in Samaria. But Jesus—knowing his coming death would rip apart the curtain in the Temple sanctuary, giving direct access for everyone to the "mercy seat" of God—knew that the real issue was far deeper than where we worship him.

Jesus wants us to trust what we cannot see and believe the one we cannot touch. Sound anything like Exodus 32?

It's that leap of faith that's always a challenge, yet always required.

All Together Now

UNDERSTANDING YOUR KIDS

Faith in the unseen usually comes more easily to kids than to adults. It's fun to watch preschoolers sort out their fairy tale friends from our ever-present God they can't see but who is still quite real. By the time little ones reach school age, they've typically got these matters down pat. Still, kids *want* to see and touch God. Although kids can imagine our God that they cannot see, they'd still love to see him face to face. And what adult wouldn't admit that there are times of doubt when we all wish God would show himself to us in a tangible way?

Kids not only want to see God, but they also want to see his Son, Jesus. A heartwarming statue of Jesus sits in the entryway of my church. It shows Jesus sitting in an inviting pose, ready to welcome children onto his lap. And kids love to scramble all over the statue. I imagine the young children in my church remember this image when they think of Jesus.

Use this lesson to help kids learn that ★ *God wants us to worship him even though we can't see him.*

THE LESSON »

ATTENTION GRABBER

Seeing What's Not There

Before class, start a frozen pizza baking in your church's kitchen. (If you're meeting in a facility without a kitchen or if the kitchen is on another floor, set up one or two toaster ovens in a room some distance from the one where you're meeting.) Time the pizza so it'll be done about 10 minutes into your teaching time.

Greet kids. Then hold up the blindfolds and say: **I'm going to ask you to trust me today. I hope you're up to that because our great adventure is about to begin!**

Have an assistant begin tying blindfolds onto the kids.

Say: **Here's the thing about these blindfolds: You're going to have a lot more fun if you can't see a thing. So as you get them tied on, help arrange them on your face for maximum darkness. If you can see, you're not going to have nearly as much fun. We want you to be able to breathe, but not see. Got that? Great!**

If your blindfold slips and you can peek out a little bit, ask for help and we'll fix it right away.

Here's what happens next. I'll put you in a line. You'll hold hands with the person in front of you and the person behind you, just like when you were little kids. Because none of you can see, I'll lead you carefully, and you'll all do your best to take care of each other. Walk in a straight line and help the people near you keep their balance. Our object is to reach our destination quickly and safely, because our destination holds a wonderful surprise.

Line up kids. Have them grasp hands, and then lead them to the door. Have your assistant stand at the end of the line. Then lead your blindfolded troop in a circuitous route to the area where the pizza is baking. Avoid having kids go on or near any stairs.

Lead the kids into a circle.

Say: **Now you're in a circle. You may drop your hands. Please do not say anything. Just raise your hands in response to my questions.**

Ask:

• **Raise your hand if you think there's no food in this room.**

• **Raise your hand if you think we're in the restroom. closet? somewhere else?**

Say: **Please hold your hands behind your back, take one**

step backward, and continue to be silent unless I ask you a question. In just a moment, someone will come around and offer you something. But keep your hands behind your back until I ask you to join hands again.

With your assistants, go around the circle slipping bites of pizza into kids' mouths. One at a time, ask kids to open their mouths. Make sure the pizza isn't too hot and the bites aren't too big. It'll take trust on the part of the kids to blindly accept what you're putting into their mouths. If some kids hesitate, pull back the pizza bite; then offer it again. Don't force a bite on anyone. Be especially aware of any allergy concerns in advance, and plan accordingly.

Move around the circle with paper towels, wiping faces as needed. Then instruct kids to take one step forward and join hands around the circle. Break the circle and lead the kids back to your room. Form a circle once more, and ask kids to take one step back and sit down. Then invite them to take off their blindfolds, and announce that it's okay to talk.

Ask:

• **What did you think of that experience?**

• **What was the most fun part?**

• **What was the scariest part?**

• **Describe what you were thinking when you got back to our room and could take off your blindfold.**

Say: **I took you out of a place you're very familiar with and asked you to go with me to a place you didn't know. God took the Israelite people out of the land of Egypt where they were slaves and asked them to follow him to a mysterious new land. They'd been living in Egypt a long time—430 years to be exact. Though their lives were hard, they knew what to expect in Egypt. In the desert following God, though, everything was strange and new.**

Ask:

• **When we got to the room where you stood in a circle, what did you think was in the room?**

• **How did not being able to see make you feel?**

• **If you did or didn't take the pizza offered to you, please explain why.**

Say: ★ *God asked the Israelites to worship him even though they couldn't see him.* **They could see the miracles he did. They could taste the food he sent them every day. But they couldn't see him the way they could see the idols and false gods in Egypt. Let's see what kind of trouble that caused in today's Bible story.**

BIBLE EXPLORATION

Aaron's Lament (Exodus 32:1-29)

Before class, arrange for a male actor in Bible-times dress to visit in the role of Aaron. Give your actor a copy of the "Aaron's Lament" script early in the week.

Say: **The problems began when God called Moses up to the holy mountain. No one knew exactly how long Moses would be on the mountain with God.**

Before Moses left, the people agreed to obey the Ten Commandments and all the other laws God gave them. The people had promised to worship God and God only. And they'd promised not to make idols.

But when Moses was up on the mountain with God— and he was up there a long time—some people forgot their promises. They went to Moses' brother Aaron and begged him to make an idol. They wanted things to be the way they'd been back in Egypt, where they saw idols all the time.

Ask:

• What do you think Aaron did—gave in to the people or stayed true to God?

Say: **I guess the only thing we can do is ask the man himself. Let's welcome Moses' brother, Aaron.**

Invite your male actor in Bible-times dress to enter the room and deliver his performance using the "Aaron's Lament" script.

Say: **Aaron was right. Moses didn't like what he saw— not one bit! Moses was carrying the stone tablets God had given him on Mount Sinai. On those tablets God had written all the laws with his own hand. But when Moses saw that the people in the camp hadn't ★** *believed in the God they couldn't see,* **he smashed the stone tablets on the mountainside in anger.**

Ask:

• Why do you think Moses was so disappointed in the people when he saw them worshipping an idol?

• What advice would you have given Aaron?

All Together Now

Aaron's Lament

> **Aaron enters and paces back and forth while he's addressing the audience. He's nervously animated and moves his hands a lot when he speaks.**

I'm sorry! I'm sorry! What more can I say? Do you know what these people are like? All 2 million or more? I always lose count. *(Stops pacing back and forth.)* It's not like I knew Moses was going to be up there on the mountain chatting with God...*(pauses for emphasis)* for 40 days. Forty days! Do you know how long that is? *(Struggles, as if trying to think of an answer.)* More than 30! Ten days longer than a month. A really, really long time, people!

> **Flustered, Aaron stops talking for a moment to regain his train of thought.**

Oh, where was I? Oh yeah, Moses went up on the holy mountain to talk to God. We didn't know how long he was going to be gone, so after a few days went by, people started to wonder where he was. A few days turned into a week. Then two weeks. The wondering turned into grumbling. Then three weeks. The grumbling got louder. Incessant. Unbearable. They came to me and said, "Where's Moses? He's been gone forever! Maybe something's happened to him. Now it's up to you to make some gods who can lead us."

Published in *All Together Now, Volume 1* by Group Publishing, Inc., 1515 Cascade Ave., Loveland, CO 80538.

101

> *Aaron shakes his head as if he can't*
> *believe what he has just heard.*

Wait. Make...gods? Me? Well, this put me in kind of a spot. There was this whole thing in God's law about not making idols, not having any other gods before him. I couldn't make a god! *(Sighs, as if giving up.)* But it's hard when nearly 2 million whiners are getting restless outside your tent.

> *Aaron crosses to the left during his next lines.*

I mean, they were looking to me to do *something*. What could I do? I didn't know when Moses was coming down. I couldn't just trot up the side of the holy mountain and say *(calls with a hand next to his mouth)* "Hey, anybody home up there? Just in case you're interested, the people are getting a little restless down here." Nooo. *(Shrugs.)* So I figured the best thing to do was give in.

> *Aaron stops walking and faces the audience.*

(Holds up hands.) I know, I know, but *you* try to make decisions when millions of people are complaining all at once! Who could put up with that, right? *(Wavers, as if making excuses.)* I was...scared. I didn't want this mob to get out of control. What good would that do? *(Winces, looking for approval from the audience.)* Right?

> *Aaron sighs again and continues.*

So I told the people to bring me some of their gold. Coins, jewelry, earrings, and other stuff. I melted down the gold and formed it into the shape of a golden calf. Back in Egypt, they worshipped a calf as the god of the Nile River. *(Holds up hands.)* It was a fake god, I knew, but I figured at least it would settle folks down for a while. *(Pauses, as if remembering how the people reacted.)* Oh boy, did the people love that golden calf! Worshipping, bowing down, singing...

Aaron shakes head and crosses back to the center.

Of course, it was wrong to worship an idol, but the people were *finally* happy. And they were leaving me alone. *(Stops and points to the left.)* And right then, wouldn't you know it, I see my brother Moses coming down off the holy mountain...*finally!* But he's *not* wearing his happy face. *(Motions as if carrying two heavy objects.)* He has these two stone tablets in his hands and he smashes them to the ground where they shatter into little pieces. And that's when I know I'm in *big* trouble.

**Aaron looks left, then right, and then speaks
with the back of his hand next to his mouth,
as if saying something "on the side."**

I don't think you wanna hear what Moses had to say to me. It's not pretty. I think I'll just wait for him over there.

Aaron takes one big step, pauses, and then quickly exits.

LIFE APPLICATION

Family Worship Challenge

Say: **God asked the people of Israel to believe in him even though they couldn't see him.**

Ask:

• **Why do you think people believe in God even though they can't see him?**

• **How have you seen God at work in your own life?**

Say: **When Jesus came to earth, he explained that God was still looking for people who would worship God not in a certain place or a certain way, but who would worship him "in spirit and in truth," which is another way of saying** ★ *God wants us to worship him even though we can't see him.*

God doesn't show himself in a body we can see; God is a spirit. Each of us has a body, a mind, and a soul or spirit. Our spirit is the part of us that loves God and speaks to him in prayer. Our spirit lives forever. So God wants us to worship him with that part of us that understands who he is and loves him.

Jesus also talked about worshipping God "in truth." In Jesus' time, some people just pretended to love God, but inside, their hearts were mean and cold. God doesn't want us to be like that. He wants people who *truly* **love him.**

That **kind of worship is a lot harder than just bowing down before some idol. It's harder than just following a bunch of rules. In fact, it's a downright challenge—a challenge I'd like you to share with your families and have fun doing it.**

First, you'll make a set of free-weight dumbbells.

Lead kids to the craft table where you've set out marshmallows, pretzel rods broken in half, copies of the "Family Worship Challenge" handout, pens, scissors, string, and resealable sandwich bags. Demonstrate how to make a dumbbell by placing a marshmallow on both ends of a pretzel rod. Have extra pretzel rods and marshmallows for munching.

Say: **Almost done! Now we'll make a little booklet to hang from your dumbbells.**

Distribute the "Family Worship Challenge" handouts. Have kids trim the edges and then fold the page in both directions to form simple four-page booklets. Have them put their names on the cover. As kids finish their booklets, use a hole punch to place a hole in the

Teacher Tip

Pressuring kids into a statement of faith that they're not yet sure of isn't the goal. Leading them gently on their own faith journey is. God makes himself known to each of us in his own time, in his own way. Be okay with just letting kids express themselves rather than telling them how they "should" think or feel.

All Together Now

Cut on outer solid lines.

• Put a sticky note on the refrigerator each time you sense that God is with you. Look at your collection together at the end of the week!

• Brainstorm one special way to worship God as a family. Will it be in a special place? At a special time?

• Jesus says that people should worship him in spirit and in truth. What does that mean to you?

• What helps you believe in God when you can't see him?

• When do you feel closest to God?

"The time is coming—indeed it's here now—when true worshipers will worship the Father in spirit and in truth. The Father is looking for those who will worship him that way. For God is Spirit, so those who worship him must worship in spirit and in truth."

John 4:23-24

Family Worship Challenge

_____

(name)

Published in *All Together Now, Volume 1* by Group Publishing, Inc., 1515 Cascade Ave., Loveland, CO 80538.

105

corner. Have kids cut a piece of string, push it through the corner hole, and then tie it around the pretzel rod so it dangles from the dumbbell.

COMMITMENT
....

Let the Challenge Begin

Say: **You've got something very exciting to take home and share with your family.**

Let's make a deal: Don't eat your dumbbell until after you've introduced your Family Worship Challenge to your family. Agreed?

Give kids each a resealable bag for storing their challenge and dumbbell.

Say: **Once you've tucked your dumbbell and booklet in the bag and sealed it, tell the person on your left when you're going to introduce the Family Worship Challenge to your family, just to remind yourself.**

CLOSING
....

Invite kids to say a closing prayer, ★ *thanking God that we can worship him even though we can't see him.*

Enough Already!

LESSON AIM

To help kids realize that ★ *God wants us to give him our best.*

OBJECTIVES

Kids will

✓ sort boxes for charity, giving reasons for their choices,

✓ role-play Israelite families deciding what to give to the Tabernacle project,

✓ make Giving Envelopes for their special project, and

✓ pray that they will give their best to God.

BIBLE BASIS

 Exodus 25:1-9; 35:20-29; 36:4-6

Here are some new and surprising insights from this trip through Exodus.

✓ It takes 15 chapters to recruit a reluctant Moses, go through the plagues, and then finally deliver the Israelites from the Egyptians at the Red Sea.

✓ Three chapters, 16 through 18, tell of the Israelites' wanderings to Mount Sinai.

✓ Six chapters, 19 through 24, are devoted to God's giving of the Covenant.

You'll need...

☐ boxes of clothes and toys to sort for keeping or giving away

☐ white trash bags

☐ permanent marker

☐ photocopy of "God's List" handout (p. 113)

☐ brochures from the international gift-giving organization of your choice

☐ photocopies of your letter to parents (sample on page 116)

☐ large glass jar

☐ photocopies of "Giving Envelope" handout (p. 117)

☐ hole punch

☐ gift ribbon

☐ scissors

☐ glue sticks

☐ Bibles

✓ The rest of the entire book—chapters 25 through 40—is concerned with building the Tabernacle and instructions for worshipping God there.

That's a big part of a very important book of Israel's history outlining in extreme detail how to build and use a "holy tent" as God's dwelling place among his people. Kind of turns your head, doesn't it? Not only are the instructions given in detail, later chapters repeat them as the craftsmen complete each task. It's obvious that God cared deeply about the careful planning and perfect execution of this project. But why?

Here we see the heart of a deeply loving God who truly wanted to be with his people. It's possible that this Tabernacle-centric focus gives us a foreshadowing of "God with us," which is eventually fulfilled and perfected in the coming of Jesus.

For this reason, we'll spend three lessons on the Tabernacle, each with a different focus. Throughout this three-week process, kids will begin to grasp the strong desire God had to *be with* his people—not only to provide for them, but also to receive their love and trust in return—perhaps to restore some of the intimacy lost in the Garden of Eden.

In today's adventure, kids will discover that ★ *God wants us to give him our best.*

📖 2 Corinthians 9:7-8

When Paul gently reminded the church at Corinth that "God loves a person who gives cheerfully," he continued a tradition that went all the way back to his (and our) ancestors in Exodus. Since God had given the people undeserved treasures, it wasn't outrageous for God to want some of them to use for his purposes.

Where might the Israelites have gotten gold and silver jewelry sufficient for making the furnishings for the Tabernacle? The fine linen, the expensively dyed cloth, the bronze?

You'll recall that on the night of the Passover, the Egyptians were so anxious for the Israelites to leave that the Egyptians readily gave them gifts—expensive gifts just like those we're speaking of here. Scripture speaks of the Israelites "plundering" Egypt. It was God's intention that his people carry all the wealth they needed to complete the beautifully appointed Tabernacle. God blessed them abundantly.

Now it was the Israelites' turn to prove themselves cheerful givers. And they gave so overwhelmingly that Moses and the workers had to beg them to stop giving—a problem many a church today would delight in, to be sure.

All Together Now

UNDERSTANDING YOUR KIDS

In truth, unless your kids have had the opportunity to visit a developing country, they've no idea of the abundance with which they're blessed. More than enough is simply the norm in North America. Sacrificial giving is not.

These passages from Exodus provide an outstanding example of how God provided the Israelites exactly what they needed so they, in turn, could give back to him. Kids can be generous in their giving to help others and show honor to God. Sometimes they can also be amazingly selfish. Help them know they're blessed by God, and giving will be more natural to them.

Use this lesson to show kids that ★ *God wants us to give him our best.* Whether it's time, talent, effort, or money, God always supplies what we need so we can keep on giving.

ATTENTION GRABBER

Keep or Toss?

Bring boxes of items to sort for charity. You might bring clothing, shoes, or kids' toys.

Say: **Millions of people buy stuff every day. Then, after a few years, they realize they have too much and aren't using a lot of it. They go through their closets and sort things to keep and to give away to charity. Sometimes it's hard for me to make these decisions, so I thought I'd ask you to help.**

Designate an area for "Keep" and an area for "Give Away."

As you go through items, point out frankly what you like or dislike about each thing. For instance, you might say, "I really like this dress—it's comfortable, it fits me well, the color looks good on me, and I wear it all the time." Or, "I bought this because I liked the style, but it doesn't fit just right so I never wear it."

Have the kids evaluate each toy: Is it working or is it broken? Does it have all the pieces or is something missing? Does the child use it or has it been outgrown? What kind of shape is the toy in— battered with missing paint or shiny and new-looking? Is the battery working?

Have kids take turns evaluating and telling you why each item should go into the Keep or Give Away pile.

Say: **I appreciate the thoughtful choices you've made. Now help me put these things into bags and mark the bags.**

Hand out the appropriate number of white garbage bags to hold the piles kids have made. Have kids mark the bags "Keep" or "Give Away." Then form a discussion circle around the bags. Pull the Give Away bags out of the circle. Draw attention to the Keep bags, and ask:

• **What might be a reason to give away these bags rather than keep them?**

• **Why do you think we can—or can't—keep the best of everything for ourselves?**

Say: **Those are tough questions. You see, most of us have plenty of stuff. We don't realize it because most of our friends have about the same amount of stuff we do. We're not bad for having plenty of stuff—not at all. That's just the way it is in our country and we can take it for granted. There are many other people in the world who have very little. But the amazing thing is a lot of these people are just as happy as we are.**

In today's Bible passage we're going to find out how
★ *God asked the Israelites to give him the very best of what they had.* The very, very best. Let's see how that turned out.

BIBLE EXPLORATION

· ·

Only the Best (Exodus 25:1-9; 35:20-29; 36:4-6)

Say: **Today I'd like your help in telling the Bible story. When I ask, "What does God want?" I want you to shout out,** ★ **"God wants us to give him our best!" Let's start where the Israelites were in front of Mount Sinai, impatient for Moses to return. They'd pestered Aaron for an idol to worship because they didn't want to wait for Moses, and they ended up getting in really big trouble with God over it. They'd disappointed God with their lack of trust. What does God want?**

Let kids shout, ★ *"God wants us to give him our best!"*

Say: **After that was all over, Moses told the people about the wonderful plans God had in mind for a holy tent. This was not just any tent—it was a special place where God would meet with his people. Usually we call this tent the Tabernacle.**

God planned every little detail of this tent. I'm going to save some of the details for next week, but believe me when I tell you this: It was absolutely beautiful. It would be God's home with the Israelites wherever they traveled. What does God want?

Let kids shout, ★ *"God wants us to give him our best!"*

Say: **Right in front of Mount Sinai, the Israelites knew God was with them. They could see smoke and fire on the mountain. They could hear thunder and feel the mountain tremble when God talked to Moses. But God's plan wasn't for the Israelites to stay at Mount Sinai. God wanted to lead them on to the Promised Land. God wanted to be with them in a way they could see and understand.**

God gave Moses a supply list so Moses could tell the Israelites everything they needed to build and furnish the Tabernacle. Take a listen.

The Lord said to Moses, "Tell the people of Israel to bring me their sacred offerings. Accept the contributions from all whose hearts are moved to offer them. Here is a list of sacred offerings you may accept from them: gold, silver, and bronze; blue, purple, and scarlet thread; fine linen and goat hair for cloth; tanned ram skins and fine goatskin leather; acacia wood; olive oil for the lamps; spices for the anointing oil and the fragrant incense; onyx stones, and other gemstones to be set in the ephod and the priest's chestpiece. Have the people of Israel build me a holy sanctuary so I can live among them. You must build this Tabernacle and its furnishings exactly according to the pattern I will show you." (Exodus 25:1-9)

What does God want?

Let kids shout, ★ *"God wants us to give him our best!"*

Ask:

• **Think of the best stuff you own. How would you feel about giving that stuff away?**

Say: **God asked the Israelites to give the very best of what they brought out of Egypt.**

The Israelites had these beautiful things because the Egyptians couldn't wait for the Israelites to leave Egypt. They wanted the Israelites out! In fact, they gave away tons of precious gifts to the Israelites and said, "Here, take these! Take anything you want. Just go!"

So the Israelites left Egypt loaded with the Egyptians' wealth—jewels, gold, silver, fine fabric—all the things God now asked from them to build the Tabernacle.

I'm not going to tell you how it turned out yet. Instead, let's form two family groups.

Point to one family. **You're the Happy-to-Give Givers.**

Point to the other family. **You're the Mumbly-Grumbly Givers.**

Choose an older child to be the father in each group, and give him or her the list of items from the "God's List" handout. Have the other group members decide who will be the mother and who the children. Say: **In your families, you'll act out the conversation that happened when the father came home with the list of things Moses requested for the Tabernacle. If you are the Happy-to-Give Givers, what would your conversation sound like? How about if you are the Mumbly-Grumbly Givers? You'll have three minutes to work together to come up with what your conversation would sound like, and then you'll present to our entire group. Remember, these are the very best items your family has, your most valuable possessions.**

All Together Now

GOD'S LIST

GOLD

SILVER

BRONZE

BLUE, PURPLE, AND SCARLET THREAD

FINE LINEN

GOAT HAIR

TANNED RAM SKINS

FINE GOATSKIN LEATHER

ACACIA WOOD

OLIVE OIL

SPICES

GEMS

GOD'S LIST

GOLD

SILVER

BRONZE

BLUE, PURPLE, AND SCARLET THREAD

FINE LINEN

GOAT HAIR

TANNED RAM SKINS

FINE GOATSKIN LEATHER

ACACIA WOOD

OLIVE OIL

SPICES

GEMS

Permission to photocopy this handout granted for local church use.
Copyright © Lois Keffer. Published in *All Together Now, Volume 1*
by Group Publishing, Inc., 1515 Cascade Ave., Loveland, CO 80538.

Help each family brainstorm as necessary. After three minutes, call time and have the two families perform. Give a round of applause for each performance.

Say: **You did a great job. Now, in your family groups, choose a volunteer to read what really happened.**

Hand out Bibles, and direct the groups to Exodus 35:20-29 and then Exodus 36:4-6.

So the whole community of Israel left Moses and returned to their tents. All whose hearts were stirred and whose spirits were moved came and brought their sacred offerings to the Lord. They brought all the materials needed for the Tabernacle, for the performance of its rituals, and for the sacred garments. Both men and women came, all whose hearts were willing. They brought to the Lord their offerings of gold—brooches, earrings, rings from their fingers, and necklaces. They presented gold objects of every kind as a special offering to the Lord. All those who owned the following items willingly brought them: blue, purple, and scarlet thread; fine linen and goat hair for cloth; and tanned ram skins and fine goatskin leather. And all who had silver and bronze objects gave them as a sacred offering to the Lord. And those who had acacia wood brought it for use in the project.

All the women who were skilled in sewing and spinning prepared blue, purple, and scarlet thread, and fine linen cloth. All the women who were willing used their skills to spin the goat hair into yarn. The leaders brought onyx stones and the special gemstones to be set in the ephod and the priest's chestpiece. They also brought spices and olive oil for the light, the anointing oil, and the fragrant incense. So the people of Israel—every man and woman who was eager to help in the work the Lord had given them through Moses—brought their gifts and gave them freely to the Lord.

(Exodus 35:20-29)

Finally the craftsmen who were working on the sanctuary left their work. They went to Moses and reported, "The people have given more than enough materials to complete the job the Lord has commanded us to do!"

So Moses gave the command, and this message was sent throughout the camp: "Men and women, don't prepare any more gifts for the sanctuary. We have enough!"

(Exodus 36:4-6)

All Together Now

When it appears both groups have read the Exodus passages, ask:

• **Why do you think the Israelites responded that way when Moses asked the people for God's list of gifts?**

Say: **Isn't that something! The Israelites brought so many gifts to the Tabernacle that Moses had to ask them to stop giving. Wow! Let's look at how ★ God asks us to give him our best.**

LIFE APPLICATION
. . . .
The Best We Have to Give

Before class, investigate various mission and charity websites. Talk to your church's missions coordinator or other church leaders to discover whether your church at large is planning to participate in a local or international outreach project. One possibility is to join in partnership with Group Cares (groupcares.org), which works with Operation Kid-to-Kid. Before you make a final decision on your gift-giving project, run it by your ministry leader. This can be a thrilling opportunity for the kids in your class to "give their best" in an entirely new way.

Say: **We've just had an entire lesson about giving our best. In just a few weeks there's a very special holiday coming up. It's the holiday when we think *most* about giving. It's the holiday when we remember that God sent *his* very best to earth in the form of a baby boy.**

Wouldn't it be great if we found a way to give someone in need our very best? Well, I've talked to some of our church leaders, and they've agreed to let us participate in a very exciting giving project.

At this point, explain and show pictures of the giving project you've chosen. Let kids know if other classes are also participating. Then set out a large glass jar.

Say: **Each week when you come, you'll have a chance to bring a special offering to God, just as the Israelites did. For our craft today, we'll make a Giving Envelope you can bring here each week. We'll tie that envelope to a letter to your parents explaining about our "very best" offering. We'll collect offerings for three weeks and put it in this jar; then we'll count our money and decide which gift we can give to someone in need.**

Giving Envelope

Before class, write a simple note to parents about your giving project, and copy it to go with the Giving Envelopes. Your note might look something like this:

Dear Moms, Dads, and Caregivers,

In our Sunday school class, we've begun a special giving project. The kids will participate with [name your organization] to purchase [name what the kids will give]. We're very excited about this and hope you will be, too!

We've just learned how the Israelites gave their very best toward the building of God's Tabernacle in the desert. We hope you and your family might contribute generously to our special project. Please help your child remember to bring the attached offering envelope for the next three Sundays.

Thanks, and God bless!

[Your name]

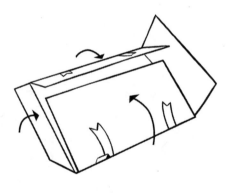

Gather kids at the craft table where you've set out copies of the "Giving Envelope" handout, scissors, glue sticks, your note to parents, brochures or printouts about your giving project, and gift ribbon.

This handout folds and glues together very simply. Have one sample cut out and folded but not glued to show kids the order in which to fold and glue it.

As kids work, punch holes in their envelopes, your notes, and information about your project. Help kids tie ribbon through the holes, making a neat package of all three items.

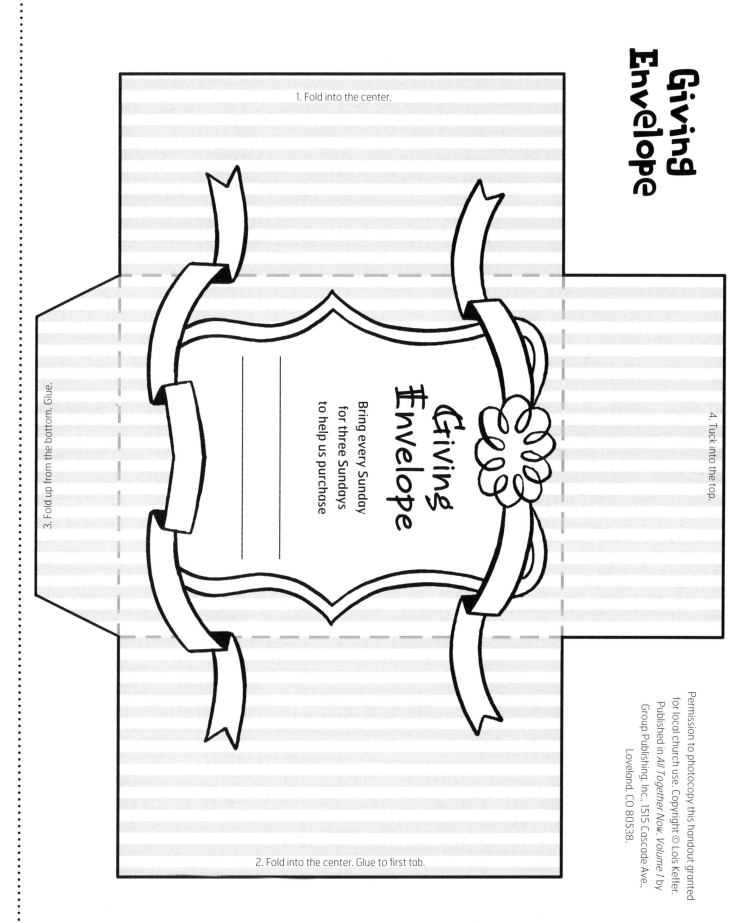

1. Fold into the center.

Giving Envelope

Bring every Sunday
for three Sundays
to help us purchase

3. Fold up from the bottom. Glue.

2. Fold into the center. Glue to first tab.

4. Tuck into the top.

CLOSING

Prayer

Gather kids in a prayer circle with their Giving Envelopes in front of them. Lead kids in prayer:

Dear Lord, help us think about giving in a new way after learning how the Israelites gave their best for the Tabernacle. We know that everything we have comes from you, so giving back is the most natural thing in the world! Teach us to show our love for you, dear God, ★ *by giving our best to you.* **In Jesus' name, amen.**

All Together Now

Building God's Holy Tent

LESSON AIM

To help kids realize that ★ *every gift God gives is special.*

OBJECTIVES

Kids will

✓ see whether they're "gifted" to meet certain challenges,

✓ choose Learning Centers to explore the building of the Tabernacle,

✓ identify special ways they might serve God in the future, and

✓ commit to using their gifts in God's service.

BIBLE BASIS

📖 **Exodus 25:8–28:42; 30:1–31:11; 35:25-26; 36:1-2; 37–38**

Many of the Israelites who traveled with Moses had learned valuable skills as slaves in Egypt—how to weave and embroider fine cloth, form and engrave precious metals, carve wood, engrave and set precious gems, and sew fine garments. These skilled workers, both male and female, were treasured in ancient societies. Today, only on rare occasions are such skills passed down from family members to younger family members as would've been the case in ancient times. Often fine handiwork today comes from overseas where labor is inexpensive.

Yet there's something honoring about putting the work of our hands into serving God. In his instructions to Moses, God

You'll need...

☐ notecards

☐ envelope

☐ 3 paper grocery bags

☐ 3 soft children's play balls

☐ 12 marshmallows*

☐ 3 resealable bags

☐ 3 sheets of paper

☐ 3 pencils

☐ whistle

☐ photocopies of "The Tabernacle" handout (p. 123)

☐ 3 photocopies of the "Learning Centers" handout (p. 125)

* Always check for allergies before serving snacks.

Note on Learning Centers: Gather the supplies only for the Learning Centers you choose to do.

Golden Lampstand

☐ gold chenille wire

☐ orange fingernail polish

☐ sharp scissors

(continued on next page)

(continued from previous page)

Embroidered Curtain

- ☐ 8-inch squares of fringed burlap
- ☐ scissors
- ☐ needles threaded with 3 strands of blue, purple, and scarlet embroidery floss cut to about 12 inches

Ark of the Covenant Model

- ☐ photocopies of the "Ark of the Covenant Model" handout (p. 126) printed on gold or yellow paper
- ☐ scissors
- ☐ glue sticks

mentions Bezalel and Oholiab as being gifted in many skills and filled with the Spirit of God for completing the great work of the Tabernacle and leading other craftsmen to help them. Can you imagine the honor of being part of such a task force?

In our society, it's people who can manipulate shares on the stock market, increase market share, or boost productivity in an organization who receive wealth and accolades. But let's not forget that God sees those who use their hands for his kingdom's sake—from making chemo caps and prayer shawls to repairing windows and plumbing and mowing lawns for those who can no longer manage on their own. These are skills that God still cherishes among his people today. They are, perhaps, the quieter gifts, but oh-so-important ones.

📖 Ephesians 2:10

Paul reminds us that God created us anew in Christ Jesus. By doing so, we are, as Paul artfully says, "God's masterpiece." I don't know about you, but there are days when I feel like anything but God's masterpiece.

Occasionally we leave a lesson exhausted, wondering if a single child took anything away from the lesson we worked so hard to prepare and teach. In this let me assure you, my friends: a "flop" of a day may just be the day God's truth takes hold in a child's life in ways you can never imagine. Keep up the great work—you may be hidden from people's view, but never from God's.

UNDERSTANDING YOUR KIDS
....

One of the greatest joys of childhood is exploration. Kids get to try their hands at different sports, various musical instruments, crafts, drama, art, and all manner of make-believe before they make their choices regarding their life's calling. Wise parents let their children "try on" a variety of activities to see what fits, without pushing the children in any particular direction until they've made choices that are truly their own. That's what the concept "a child's work is his or her play" is all about.

This story of the Tabernacle helps kids see that each of us is uniquely gifted for God's service. The learning centers in this lesson allow kids to "dip a toe" in different types of skills.

All Together Now

ATTENTION GRABBER

Family Challenges

Before class, write each of these challenges on separate notecards.

- ✓ *spin a ball on your finger*
- ✓ *balance a bag of marshmallows on your nose*
- ✓ *hum a note longer than anyone else*
- ✓ *draw a perfect square*

Place the notecards in an envelope, and keep the envelope with you.

Place three large paper grocery bags in front of you. To each bag add:

- ✓ *a child's soft play ball*
- ✓ *4 marshmallows in a sealed bag*
- ✓ *a sheet of paper*
- ✓ *a pencil*

Tell kids that they're going to have some Tabernacle fun today. Form three family groups by having them count off by threes. You'll have three family groups. It doesn't matter if family groups have equal numbers of kids. Have each family group sit in a circle; then send a member of each family to pick up one paper grocery bag. Tell families not to look inside the bag.

Say: **When I announce a task, two family members from each group get to feel inside the bag for what they need to perform the task. As a family, you get to decide which two people from your group will perform the task.**

Choose a task card from your envelope and read it aloud.

Say: Feel inside your bag for the item or items you need to complete that task. Don't start until I blow my whistle; keep trying until I blow my whistle again. Families, don't forget to cheer for each other.

Allow time for families to find what they need to accomplish the chosen task. When everyone is ready, blow the whistle. Cheer loudly as the participants do their best to accomplish their challenges. Allow no more than 30 seconds, and then blow the whistle to stop.

Have families choose their next participants; then read the next task to everyone. Proceed as before with everyone cheering for all participants. Repeat this until you've done all the tasks.

At the close of the family challenges, allow families to eat the marshmallows. Then collect the paper bags, gather everyone in a large circle, and ask:

- **Which was the most fun challenge to watch?**
- **How'd you do at your challenge?**
- **Explain whether you think you would've been better at a different challenge.**

Say: **Some of you wish you'd have gotten a different challenge, and some of you are happy with the challenge you got. Our game showed us how we're able to do some things better than others. But it's not that anyone is better than anyone else; this shows us how God has gifted us with different talents.**

Today we're going to learn that ★ *every gift God gives is special.* For building the Tabernacle, God gave special gifts to some very amazing people.

BIBLE EXPLORATION

. . . .

Exploring the Tabernacle (Exodus 25:8—28:42; 30:1—31:11; 35:25-26; 36:1-2; 37—38)

Say: **When Moses was on the mountain with God, God laid out very precise plans for how he wanted the Tabernacle built, what materials he wanted the Israelites to use, and how he wanted each piece of furniture constructed and used. And God's people gave their very best so the Tabernacle could be built.**

God's people brought their finest things for the Tabernacle: fine linen, scarlet and purple cloth, goat hair, animal skins, jewels, gold, silver, and bronze.

Say: **God told Moses exactly what size he wanted everything to be and what designs he wanted included. Fortunately, Moses didn't have to remember everything because God said there were two craftsmen named Bezalel and Oholiab who were gifted to do all this work, and God's Spirit would help them. Let's walk through the Tabernacle and take a look at the jobs they had to do.**

The Tabernacle was a tent surrounded by a large courtyard. God gave instructions for four pieces of furniture to be placed inside the tent. Let's look first at the table

Teacher Tip

When kids try to draw a perfect square, compare the squares, compliment them all, and announce that no one can draw a perfect square without a ruler.

All Together Now

The Tabernacle

The Ark of the Covenant

The Incense Altar

The Lampstand

The Table for the Bread of the Presence

Published in *All Together Now, Volume 1* by Group Publishing, Inc., 1515 Cascade Ave., Loveland, CO 80538.

123

where bread would be placed. The table was made of wood and covered with gold. Priests made 12 loaves of bread—called the Bread of the Presence—and placed them in two rows on the table. They represented the 12 tribes of Israel.

Next came the lampstand. It was made of one piece of solid gold! It had one column straight up the middle and three branches going out each side. Today we call candlesticks that look like this menorahs. It was the priests' job to keep the lamps lit day and night. The light from these candles lit the bread on the opposite side of the tent.

In the middle, right in front of the curtain that divided the tent, stood the incense altar. Priests kept fragrant incense burning to God.

Then came a curtain that divided the tent in two. Only one piece of furniture stood in the back part of the tent: the Ark of the Covenant. It was a big box that contained the Ten Commandments, a jar of manna, and Aaron's staff. The high priest only went into the back part of the tent, the Most Holy Place, once a year to make a sacrifice for the people's sin. The Ark of the Covenant would be God's throne on earth!

So there's our quick walk through the Tabernacle. Now you get to make your own Tabernacle souvenir, working like the craftspeople who built the Tabernacle!

LIFE APPLICATION
. . . .
Tabernacle Learning Centers

Let kids choose one, two, or all three of the Learning Centers. Kids love choices, and each center requires very few materials. Copy the "Learning Centers" handout, and place two or three copies of the instructions at each center along with the needed supplies.

COMMITMENT
. . . .
Works of Art

Let kids work at the Learning Centers as long as time allows. Blow your whistle for a two-minute warning when it's time to clean up. Then bring everyone together and let them share and comment on their works of art.

All Together Now

Learning Centers

Golden Lampstand

Supplies: gold chenille wire, orange fingernail polish, sharp scissors (provide adult assistance with these)

God said to create the golden lampstand from solid gold. One piece went straight up the middle. Six arms branched out from the middle—three on each side. It was the priests' job to keep the seven lamps burning day and night.

How will you create your lampstand? When you've finished, brush a tiny bit of orange nail polish on top of each branch to represent the flame.

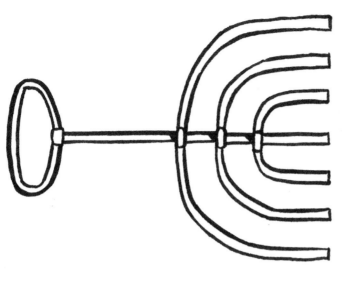

Embroidered Curtain

Supplies: 8-inch squares of burlap, scissors, needles threaded with three strands of blue, purple, and scarlet embroidery floss cut to about 12 inches (Have an adult to help younger kids with this project.)

The courtyard of the Tabernacle was surrounded by curtains hanging on poles. Curtains made the inside layer of the four layers of the tent itself. And a special curtain hung in the center of the tent to separate the Ark of the Covenant from where the priests went every day to tend the lamps and the incense and the Bread of the Presence.

God chose these colors for decorating the curtains. Stitch across the bottom of your curtain. Make simple, large stitches.

Ark of the Covenant Model

Supplies: copies of the "Ark of the Covenant Model" handout on gold or yellow paper, scissors, glue sticks

The Ark of the Covenant stood alone in the Holy of Holies—the back part of the Tabernacle tent where the high priest entered only once a year. The Ark would be God's throne on earth. It was made of wood and covered inside and out with gold.

Moses placed three important reminders of God's care inside the Ark: (1) the tablets containing the Ten Commandments, (2) Aaron's staff, and (3) a jar of manna.

Follow the instructions on the handout to make your very own model of the Ark of the Covenant.

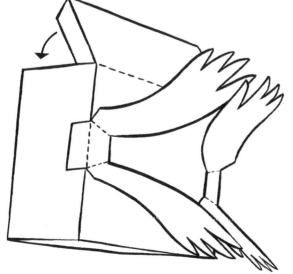

Ark of the Covenant Model

1. Cut roughly around the wings. Fold them in half to cut them out precisely.
2. Cut out the box on the solid lines. Fold it down on the dotted lines. Run glue stick around the tabs and fold the box together.
3. Put glue on the drop-down tab of the wings and attach them to the ends of the box.
4. Fold the wings forward so they cover the box.

Ask:

• **Describe what you liked best about these projects.**

• **What do you think it was like for God's people to have such an awesome job to do for God?**

• **If you could've had any job to help create the Tabernacle, what would you do and why?**

• **What kinds of craftspeople serve our church today?**

Say: **Today, there are lots of people who don't know about woodworking or setting jewels or weaving fabric or working with gold like people in Moses' time did. Instead, we serve God in different ways, like the people who serve our church today. And ★ *every gift God gives is special.***

Ask:

• **What kinds of skills do people use to serve God today?**

• **What are some ways you could start using your gifts to serve God?**

Say: **In their own way, the people we just talked about use their skills to build God's church, just as the craftspeople of old built God's Tabernacle. How cool is that! What's even cooler is that ★ *every gift God gives is special.***

CLOSING

Hearts and Hands to God

Gather kids in a tight circle for a closing prayer. Have kids hold their hands out, palms up. Lead them in this prayer:

Dear God, it's been incredible to learn about the skilled work that went into the building of your Tabernacle. We believe that you have given each of us special skills to make your kingdom grow. Help us commit those skills to serving you with all our hearts. In Jesus' name we pray, amen.

The Tabernacle and Jesus' Sacrifice

You'll need...

- ☐ extra adult helper
- ☐ area to wash hands (or use hand sanitizer)
- ☐ one 4- to 6-inch wide strip of cloth for each child to use as a belt; a variety of colors is fine
- ☐ large toaster oven
- ☐ silver (or foil covered) tray
- ☐ 2 small tables
- ☐ silver (or foil covered) bowl
- ☐ refrigerator biscuits*
- ☐ incense made with frankincense and myrrh *or* a scented candle
- ☐ 7 battery-powered tea lights
- ☐ sheets of paper
- ☐ Bibles
- ☐ lighter
- ☐ bottle of liquid smoke barbecue sauce
- ☐ photocopies of the "I Am" handout (p. 135)
- ☐ scissors
- ☐ glue sticks
- ☐ "Sacred Shabbat" from Loreena McKennitt's album *An Ancient Muse* or "Egypt Soundtrack" from Group's Egypt VBS (available at group.com), or other thoughtful instrumental music *(optional)*
- ☐ CD player

* Always check for allergies before serving snacks.

LESSON AIM

To help kids learn that ★ *Jesus is the perfect, once-and-for-all sacrifice for our sins.*

OBJECTIVES

Kids will

- ✓ put the elements of the outer court of the Tabernacle in place,
- ✓ experience the duties of a Tabernacle priest,
- ✓ learn how Jesus made one sacrifice for all, and
- ✓ thank Jesus for his perfect sacrifice for our sins.

BIBLE BASIS

 Exodus 39:32—40:36

With months of hard work finally complete, Moses had the Tabernacle erected exactly one year after the first Passover. Immediately God's presence filled the tent to the point that even Moses himself could not enter. Interestingly, the word *tabernacle* means "to dwell with." Finally God had a traveling home with his people, a home where they could experience his presence day and night, a home that would go with them in all their travels. When the cloud of God's presence stayed upon the tent, the Israelites stayed where they were; when it lifted, they moved on.

The priests kept the lamps glowing day and night. Every Sabbath they placed new bread on the table and ate the old,

All Together Now

which was as fresh to them as the day it was baked.

The people didn't gather around the Tabernacle on the Sabbath except during the special holidays God declared. For the Israelites in the desert, Sabbath meant resting in their tents, not going to a place of worship as we do today. That practice began much later.

When God's presence fell on and filled the Tabernacle, awe must've also filled the hearts not only of the craftspeople who worked on it, but of the entire community of Israelites. Rather than an idol made of gold, the people had the dwelling place of the living God who'd brought them out of slavery, shown them his mighty power, cared for them daily, and called them his own, and who now made his throne on earth among them.

📖 Hebrews 9:1-12

By the time the book of Hebrews was written, the Tabernacle was a very distant memory for the Jews and a completely foreign idea to the Gentiles. The writer of Hebrews had to summarize what the Tabernacle looked like and how it worked before he could make the analogy of Jesus as the High Priest. Like many things in the Exodus journey of the Israelites, Tabernacle worship points an arrow directly to our Savior, Jesus. No more do we need sacrifices of lambs, goats, or cows. Jesus, whom John the Baptist called the lamb of God, became the one perfect lamb, the last sacrifice for all time. No longer would there need to be a Tabernacle or a Temple or any other solitary place where God resided in the Most Holy Place. Instead, Christ has "entered the Most Holy Place once for all time and secured our redemption forever" (Hebrews 9:12).

UNDERSTANDING YOUR KIDS

This lesson appeals to your kids' various senses and incorporates several ways kids can learn. These different experiences are designed to engage kids who learn in different ways. So rather than just listening to a teacher talk, kids get to use touch, sight, sound, relationships, and more. We'll ask kids to take a big jump in understanding when we take them from the Tabernacle sacrifices to the last and perfect sacrifice Jesus made on the cross. Your kids can make this mental bridge when you lay the groundwork for understanding throughout the lesson and tap their senses and interests to keep them engaged. Keep this in mind as you "spin the plates" of different experiences, and point out significant connections between the Old Testament and New Testament with your kids.

THE LESSON »

ATTENTION GRABBER

The Holy Place

This activity will be more effective if you can bake the biscuits in a toaster oven in your meeting room. If that is not possible, bring freshly baked biscuits or small loaves of bread and allow kids to smell and taste them.

Say: **God gave the Israelites very specific instructions on how to build the Tabernacle, which would serve as God's dwelling place among his people. His instructions were specific, all the way down to what patterns should be on the furniture. And finally, after all that work, the Israelites finished the Tabernacle. Moses and the priests put the entire thing together. Now you get the privilege of going into the tent—something no one but the priests could do. And you'll get to do some of the jobs only the priests did. Pretty amazing!**

The priests had to go through an elaborate ritual of cleansing before they could enter the tent. To symbolize that, we'll wash our hands.

Have kids wash their hands at a sink or washbowl, or pass a bottle of hand sanitizer around. You may wish to play some thoughtful instrumental music during this time, such as "Sacred Shabbat" from Loreena McKennitt's album *An Ancient Muse* or the "Egypt Soundtrack" from Group's Egypt VBS. Replay the track as work continues. Stop the music when you gather in a circle to talk.

Say: **The priests had special garments they wore only for serving in the Tabernacle. They were woven from the finest linen. I don't have linen garments for each of you, but I do have belts that you can wear—and keep—to represent the special clothing the priests wore in the Tabernacle.**

Present your belts. Let each child choose one and put it on.

Say: **Now we're ready to get started with priestly jobs.**

Our first job is to get the Bread of the Presence ready. One family alone was responsible for this bread, and only they knew just how to do it. For today, we'll use biscuits to symbolize our Bread of the Presence.

Choose a couple of kids to open the biscuits and get them ready to put into the toaster oven. Assure kids that there will be plenty of jobs for all.

Say: **Okay, now we'll be able to smell the sweet scent of bread as we go on with our work.**

All Together Now

There were always 12 loaves of the Bread of the Presence in the Tabernacle. The 12 loaves represented the 12 tribes of Israel.

Those of you who helped with the bread are responsible for watching it and making sure we take it out when it's light golden brown. Have an adult keep an eye on the biscuits, too.

BIBLE EXPLORATION
••

Symbols of Christ (Exodus 39:32–40:36)

Say: **Inside the Tabernacle, the golden lampstand and the Bread of the Presence table faced each other. They were the first things you would've encountered inside the tent. The incense altar was placed farther back in the middle, right in front of the curtain that divided the tent and hid the back part that contained the Ark of the Covenant.**

Form three teams with the kids who didn't help with the bread: the Bread of the Presence Table Crew, the Golden Lampstand Crew, and the Incense Altar Crew. A team can be one child. Give each team the following instructions.

Say: **Bread of the Presence Table Crew, place a small table over here** (indicate placement)**, and put a tray on it for when the bread is ready.**

Say: **Golden Lampstand Crew, line up the seven tea lights over here** (point out a high, sturdy surface opposite the bread) **and turn them on.**

Say: **Incense Altar Crew, place the other small table here** (indicate placement)**, and place the silver bowl on top of it. Inside the bowl, place the frankincense and myrrh incense** [or the scented candle]**.** Light the incense or candle and put the lighter away.

By this time the biscuits in the toaster oven may be ready. Have the Bread of the Presence Crew take the silver tray to the toaster oven where the kids who prepared the biscuits, with adult help, can place the warm bread on the silver tray. The Bread of the Presence Crew will then return the tray to the table.

Darken your room, stop the music, and have everyone join you in a circle in the middle of your re-creation of the Holy Place.

Say: **We're in the just-finished Tabernacle. Before too long Moses and the priests will dedicate everything with oil and invite God to come into the very tent that he designed** for himself, that the Israelites gave gifts for, that crafts-people worked on for months. But right now, it's just us. This tent and its outer courtyard aren't too far from Mount Sinai, the mountain of God, where Moses goes up to talk to God; the mountain that shakes with fire and smoke and bolts of lightning when God speaks.

We're in a hot, hot desert, but the four layers of covering over this tent make it cooler inside. There may be a desert breeze.

Give kids sheets of paper to fan for a "desert" breeze.

Say: Outside in the outer court, other priests are preparing sacrifices. They choose the strongest and healthiest animals to be killed on the altar and then offered as sacrifices for sins, just the way God told Moses. Certain parts are roasted on the open fire. It smells delicious. While we don't know exactly how the smoke smelled, it was probably something like this. Open a bottle of liquid smoke barbecue sauce, and pass it around for kids to smell. So now you can add barbecued meat to the things you smell. Priests will bring hot coals from the fire into this room and mix them with the incense in the bowl to keep it burning all the time.

Remember, this tent has no windows, so even though there's bright desert light outside, this room is lit only by candlelight and the glow of burning incense.

Ask:

• What do you think was God's purpose for having the people build this special place of worship?

• How is the place we've created today like or not like the church buildings we use today?

Say: The priests in the Tabernacle actually ate the Bread of the Presence when they changed it before each Sabbath. So pass it around and let's each enjoy some.

Take a few moments to enjoy the bread.

Say: You'd think week-old bread would be stale and dry. But when the priests placed the new loaves on the tray, the old loaves they ate were as fresh as the new ones.

Now I'm going to let you in on a great truth about Jesus and the Tabernacle. Let's do a little digging with our crews to find out what this great truth is. Distribute Bibles to crews. Working in groups, have kids read Exodus 39:32–40:36 and then Hebrews 9:1-12. Have crews report what the truth is about Jesus and the Tabernacle. After all crews have reported, say: All the things you see and smell and taste around you point straight

All Together Now

to the New Testament and Jesus' time on earth, more than a thousand years later. ★ *Jesus is the perfect, once-and-for-all sacrifice for our sins.* But for now, let's get back to the Tabernacle.

When the Tabernacle was all ready, Moses dedicated all the parts of the Tabernacle. He did this by "anointing," which means he spread an oil that God told him to prepare on those Tabernacle places. Then something amazing happened. Here's what the Bible says:

> *Then the cloud covered the Tabernacle, and the glory of the Lord filled the Tabernacle. Moses could no longer enter the Tabernacle because the cloud had settled down over it, and the glory of the Lord filled the Tabernacle. (Exodus 40:34-35)*

Say: **Just imagine the sights and sounds when God's glory came swooshing down and covered the Tabernacle and filled it.**

LIFE APPLICATION
Old to New

Before class, assemble an "I Am" handout for the kids to examine in this activity.

Say: **A moment ago I told you that Jesus was connected to everything around us. We've been enjoying the Bread of the Presence. Listen to these words of Jesus:**

> *I am the bread of life. Whoever comes to me will never be hungry again. Whoever believes in me will never be thirsty. (John 6:35)*

Jesus said this right after he fed 5,000 people from one little boy's shared lunch. But Jesus wanted them to know that he wasn't going to give them ordinary bread. He told them that he was the living bread that came down from heaven. That reminded everyone of the manna that fell in the wilderness. That's the bread connection.

Listen again to Jesus' words:

> *I am the light of the world. If you follow me, you won't have to walk in darkness, because you will have the light that leads to life. (John 8:12)*

Jesus said this before healing a blind man. As I mentioned before, the flames on the golden lampstand were the only light in the Tabernacle. Jesus came to light the way straight to God. Because of the sacrifice he was going to make, there'd be no more need for a lampstand or special sacrifices or ceremonies. People who believe in Jesus can find their way straight to God without all these things.

Listen to these words spoken about Jesus:

Look! The Lamb of God who takes away the sin of the world.
(John 1:29)

John the Baptist spoke these words when he saw Jesus. And these are perhaps the most important words of all. Do you remember that we talked about animals—bulls, goats, and lambs—being sacrificed for sins outside the tent? Jesus came and lived a perfect life, and he willingly sacrificed his life on the cross. His blood became the one perfect sacrifice for all time, forever.

We no longer need the Tabernacle and all its ceremonies. Jesus is the only high priest we'll ever need. He has opened the way for us to come to God directly, on our own. Let's put this handout together, and it will show you exactly what I mean. First we'll set all the Tabernacle pieces aside to show that we don't need them anymore.

Gather kids around a craft table where you've set out the "I Am" handouts, scissors, and glue sticks. Lead kids through the following instructions for assembling the handout.

1. Cut around the entire figure, and then cut it into two pieces on the heavy line.
2. Turn the pieces over so the blank sides face you. Place the larger piece on top of the smaller one. Glue the centers together.
3. Still with the blank sides facing you, fold the page with the cloud picture forward and glue it to the blank center page. Then fold the Lamb of God page forward.
4. Fold the bread of life page forward; then the light of the world page.

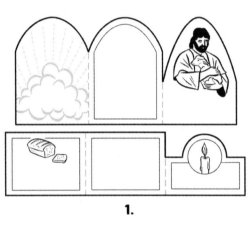

1.

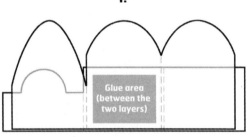

Glue area (between the two layers)

2.

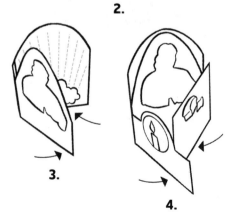

3.

4.

All Together Now

I Am

"I am the light of the world."
(John 8:12)

"We can boldly enter heaven's Most Holy Place because of the blood of Jesus. By his death, Jesus opened a new and life-giving way through the curtain into the Most Holy Place...let us go right into the presence of God with sincere hearts."
(Hebrews 10: 19–22)

"I am the bread of life."
(John 6:35)

"The Lamb of God who takes away the sin of the world."
(John 1:29)

COMMITMENT

. . . .

Our High Priest

Have kids gather with their completed handouts in the story circle.

Say: **Pretty cool how this works, isn't it? We can go through page by page and see how Jesus fulfilled every purpose of the Tabernacle. He's the Bread of Life, the Light of the World, and the Lamb of God who takes away the sins of the world. Let's turn to the cloud picture and see what else Jesus does.**

Ask a willing child to read the verse.

Say: **In the time of the Tabernacle, the priests sacrificed animals and sprinkled blood against the altar to obtain the forgiveness of sins. But Jesus willingly sacrificed himself so that people's sins could be forgiven once and for all. If we put our faith in Jesus, our sins are forgiven—period.**

The High Priest went into the Most Holy Place only once a year to atone for the sins of the people. Now Jesus is our High Priest. He's the High Priest in heaven. He's always pleading our case to God. The curtain that once kept the Most Holy Place from view is gone. Jesus invites us right into the throne room of God.

CLOSING

. . . .

Prayer of Faith

Say: **Thousands of years after the Tabernacle, it's sometimes hard to imagine how the Israelites worshipped there. Today, we've looked at the sights, smells, and tastes of how the Tabernacle worked. We've also learned how through his death and life, Christ Jesus became the perfect sacrifice for all time. Let's pray a thank-you to Jesus for that wonderful gift.**

Dear Lord Jesus, thank you for dying for us and being the perfect sacrifice for our sins. Thank you for living again and being our great High Priest in heaven. We love you. Amen.

All Together Now

Exodus Journeys

LESSON AIM

To help kids remember that ★ *God leads us to grow closer to him.*

OBJECTIVES

Kids will

✓ decorate for a party and sing "Pharaoh, Pharaoh,"

✓ review the book of Exodus with an Exodus Journey,

✓ examine how God has been a part of their own life journey, and

✓ tell what "Exodus souvenirs" they've taken to heart.

BIBLE BASIS

 Exodus 3:7-12

Exodus begins with a runaway prince encountering God alone on a mountainside. It ends gloriously with the freed nation of Israel spread out in a great encampment set a respectful distance from that mountain, celebrating the dedication of the Tabernacle. From a nation enslaved, the Israelites became a nation delivered and beloved. A year from the date of the Passover, God filled the Tabernacle with his holy presence, establishing the covenant he'd so carefully worked out with his people during the intervening months.

What a saga—the birth of a reluctant nation who required the wooing of miracle after miracle. Their lives in Egypt, while

You'll need...

☐ party decorations

☐ doughnut holes*

☐ "Pharaoh, Pharaoh" (you can download the Butterfly Kids version at iTunes.com)

☐ CD player

☐ 4 signs on 11x17 paper: "Egypt," "The Red Sea," "Mount Sinai," and "The Wilderness"

☐ kid-friendly Bibles, such as the *Hands-On Bible* from Group (group.com)

☐ photocopies of the "My Life Journey" handout (p. 143)

☐ paper

☐ pencils, pens, crayons, stickers, and other decorative materials

* Always check for allergies before serving snacks.

harsh, were their lives. Things were familiar, routine, to be done without thinking. What did God offer them? Change. A new identity. The opportunity to be his chosen people, beloved above all others on earth. Adventure. To set out across the desert with a host of millions, to find their way to a bountiful land flowing with milk and honey, to take that land in the name of the living God, and to live and prosper there with their families for generations to come.

In times of great change, many of us are yanked away from what's expected and familiar. We never know when God may pull us into a wilderness experience of our own. It won't be comfortable. It won't take us through familiar territory. There will be times when we will find ourselves like Moses, on our faces before God. But know this: God always brings us back around. His Word is solid, his promises true. And during our wilderness times, we'll know him more intimately than ever before.

📖 **Hebrews 9:11–12**

Through Jesus, we celebrate the new covenant perfected once and for all and a high priest who understands what we're made of and who constantly pleads our case before God.

Exodus is about redemption. God worked mightily to redeem the people of Israel from slavery and draw them into a covenant relationship. After working through Exodus, you owe yourself a cup of hot cider and a read through Hebrews. It will sing to your soul as never before.

UNDERSTANDING YOUR KIDS

What a great teacher you are! In completing these lessons on Exodus, you've taken your kids on a journey in spiritual formation that many adults have never experienced. At the same time you've built a foundation in biblical literacy that your kids will not soon forget. Having this chance to reprocess and review is golden. Reinforcement is one of the keys to entrenching knowledge deep into long-term memory.

The Israelites were pursued by God, failed him, and were brought back once more throughout this marvelous book. Isn't that the story of all of us? How awesome for kids to know that throughout their lives, God will be "after them" with his love, and that Jesus, their all-knowing high priest, has opened the way to God for them.

All Together Now

ATTENTION GRABBER

"Pharaoh, Pharaoh" Party

Greet kids with a box of party decorations and a box of doughnut holes.

Say: **Today we're going to celebrate everything you've learned about the book of Exodus with a party. Let's see how quickly you can get our room party-ready. Of course, you'll need fuel for the job, so here are some doughnut holes to get you started.**

Play lively music as you help kids decorate for the party. Post the 11x17 signs for the Bible Exploration Journey in four corners of your room: "Egypt," "Mount Sinai," "The Red Sea," and "The Wilderness." Arrange the signs so when you lead kids to them, they'll have to criss-cross the room to find the chronological order.

Say: **Thanks for helping decorate! Let's give ourselves a big cheer!**

Lead kids in a round of wild cheers, and then motion for quiet.

Say: **Now let's get this party rollin' with the greatest Exodus song ever—"Pharaoh, Pharaoh"!**

Cue "Pharaoh, Pharaoh" and play it loudly. If kids love it, play it again.

Say: **That song is a fun way to tell the Exodus passages about Moses and Pharaoh. But Exodus is also about many other major truths about how ★ *God leads us to grow closer to him.* Let's take a short journey back through Exodus to show how God journeyed with the Israelites and with us, too.**

> ## Teacher Tip
>
> Make sure kids of all ages get to put up decorations. The goal isn't beauty—it's that everyone gets to participate.

BIBLE EXPLORATION

Exodus Journey (Exodus 1–40)

Say: **Today's party includes a road trip. The book of Exodus tells about a journey of God's people—not just "way back then" but also today, for us. Today we're going to take this amazing journey back through Exodus. Along the way, we'll look into the Bible to see what's happened there. Let's get going! Our first stop is in Egypt.**

Lead kids to the corner of the room with the "Egypt" sign.

Say: **This is where it all began—in Egypt. Let's take a look at what happened in Egypt. To do that, we'll travel in teams.**

Each team will read its passage and then report back to the entire group what it's learned. Your team can tell us about the passage, draw an illustration, or re-enact it. We'll move fast, so work together quickly and keep your reports simple.

Form three teams, asking for a child to volunteer to read in each team. A team can be one child, so provide reading assistance if necessary. Assign one passage to each of the three teams.

1. The Israelites are forced into slavery and Moses is born: Exodus 1:1-14 and Exodus 2:1-10.

2. Moses is called to lead the people out of Egypt: Exodus 3.

3. Israel's escape from Egypt: Exodus 12:31-42.

Give teams time to read their passages and prep their reports. Then gather everyone's attention and ask teams to offer their reports in order.

When all three groups have finished, say: **Great job! Now let's keep moving on our road trip. Next stop, the Red Sea.**

Lead the group to the corner of the room marked with the sign "The Red Sea."

Assign one passage to each of the three teams.

1. Israel detours through the wilderness: Exodus 13:17-14:4.

2. Egyptians pursue Israel: Exodus 14:5-14.

3. Israel escapes through the Red Sea: Exodus 14:15-31.

Give teams time to read their passages and prep their reports. Ask teams to use a different method to report back to the group this time. Then gather everyone's attention and let teams share, again in order.

When teams are finished, say: **Let's keep moving on our road trip. Next stop, the Wilderness.**

Lead the group to the corner of the room marked with the sign "The Wilderness."

Assign one passage to each of the three teams.

1. Bitter water at Marah: Exodus 15:22-27.

2. Manna and quail from heaven: Exodus 16.

3. Jethro's advice to Moses: Exodus 18:13-27.

Give teams time to read their passages and prep their reports. Ask them to use the method they haven't used yet to retell what happened. Then gather everyone's attention and ask teams to offer their reports in order.

When all three groups have finished, thank teams for their reports and say: **Now let's keep moving on our road trip. This will be our final stop, at Mount Sinai.**

Lead the group to the corner of the room marked with the sign "Mount Sinai." Assign one passage to each of the three teams.

All Together Now

1. Moses climbs up and down Mount Sinai: Exodus 19.

2. God gives the Ten Commandments: Exodus 20:1-17.

3. The people worship God in the Tabernacle near Mount Sinai: Exodus 40.

Give teams time to read their passages and prep their reports. Tell them they can use any method they'd like to retell the story this time. Then gather everyone's attention and ask teams to offer their reports in order.

Gather everyone in a circle in the middle of your room.

Say: **We've just made a whirlwind tour through Exodus. What happened to the Israelites shows us ★ *God leads us to grow closer to him.***

Ask:

• **How was moving around like the Israelites' journey?**

• **Why did God send the people of Exodus on a long journey rather than quickly moving them from Egypt to the Promised Land as he could've done?**

Say: **The distance from Egypt to the Promised Land really isn't that far. God could've made the journey really fast and efficient. Instead, God made the journey difficult and it lasted 40 years. That's because ★ *God leads us to grow closer to him.* Let's look at what that means.**

LIFE APPLICATION
. . . .

My Faith Journey

Before class make a copy of the "My Life Journey" handout for each child.

Say: **You may've heard the saying, "Life is a journey." That's true for everyone, and it was certainly true for Moses and the people of Israel. Let's take a few minutes to dream about our own life journeys—where we've been, where we are, and where we want to go.**

Distribute a copy of the "My Life Journey" handout to each child. Have available pens, pencils, crayons, stickers, and other decorative materials for kids to use to create their life journeys.

Say: **On your handouts, write or draw the main events so far in your life in the "Where I've Been" column, such as where and when you were born, where you first lived, and important things that've happened in your life so far. You** can write, draw, and decorate however you wish. You'll have four minutes to do this.

Give kids time to create their "Where I've Been" columns; then gather everyone's attention.

Say: **In the "Where I Am" column, write or draw things that are happening in your life now, such as where you live, who you live with, where you go to school, what you like to do, and so on.**

Give kids four minutes to create their "Where I Am" columns; then gather everyone's attention.

Say: **In the "Where I'm Going" column, write or draw things that you want to do or become someday.**

Give kids four minutes to create their "Where I'm Going" columns; then gather everyone's attention.

Say: **Find a partner. Partners, tell each other all about yourselves.**

Give pairs a few minutes to share their lives with each other. Halfway through the time, remind kids to let their partners talk. Then gather everyone's attention.

Ask:

• **What things did you learn or remember about yourself by creating your life journey?**

• **Where have you seen God at work in your life journey so far?**

Say: **All of us are on a journey in life. We've seen in Exodus that God wanted more than anything to lead the people and to journey with them through all things. The same ★** *God leads us to grow closer to him.* **God has been with you since the beginning, is with you now, and wants to journey with you for the rest of your life.**

COMMITMENT
. . . .

Exodus Souvenirs

Say: **Wow—this has been a really busy party!**

Before we finish, I'd like to have a moment for you to think. Let's think about this: The book of Exodus teaches us a lot about God.

Ask:

• **What have you learned about God as we've studied the book of Exodus?**

All Together Now

My Life Journey

Where I've Been ▾

Where I Am ▾

Where I'm Going ▾

• What was the most surprising thing you've learned about God in the book of Exodus?

• Tell about a souvenir you have from someplace special you've been.

If you have childhood souvenirs, talk about them as well.

Say: **It's fun to have souvenirs of special times and places we've visited. But guess what? You also just told me about your souvenirs from God's Word when you told me about what you've learned and what surprised you about Exodus. You told me things such as** [repeat what the children shared earlier]. **These are** *heart* **souvenirs. They'll shape you as you grow. They're planted deep inside you, protected by the Holy Spirit, who helped put them there. Nothing can take them away from you.**

I'm so glad we made this journey through Exodus together!

CLOSING

Prayer

Close in a prayer similar to this one.

Dear God, we've been with your people as they suffered and slaved away in the hot sun of Egypt. We've watched your mighty power in the plagues. We've trembled with your people as the mighty Egyptian army advanced and they were trapped against the Red Sea. We've marveled as the sea stood up in walls and your people walked through on dry ground, and then we cheered as the sea swallowed up the enemy. Through all our journeys in Exodus, we've learned that ★ *God leads us to grow closer to him.* **We praise you, Lord! In Jesus' name, amen.**

All Together Now